Exploring

Understanding Self through Journaling to enhance Modeling and Experientially teaching Character Concepts to Children

DR. SHIRLEY B. MCNEILL

Outskirts Press, Inc.
Denver, Colorado

The opinions expressed in this manuscript are solely the opinions of the author and do not represent the opinions or thoughts of the publisher.

Exploring Sensational YOU
Understanding Self through Journaling to enhance Modeling and Experientially teaching Character Concepts to Children All Rights Reserved
Copyright © 2007 Dr. Shirley B. McNeill
V 4.0

This book may not be reproduced, transmitted, or stored in whole or in part by any means, including graphic, electronic, or mechanical without the express written consent of the publisher except in the case of brief quotations embodied in critical articles and reviews.

Outskirts Press
http://www.outskirtspress.com

ISBN-10: 1-4327-0279-3
ISBN-13: 978-1-4327-0279-3

Outskirts Press and the "OP" logo are trademarks belonging to Outskirts Press, Inc.

Printed in the United States of America

PREFACE

Parenting has been the most difficult chore in my life and at the same time it has given me more joy than any other life accomplishment. I am honored to have experienced the ups and downs of parenting, the growth, acquiring and effectively pursuing new skills. I am also grateful for the opportunity to give someone all the things I received and did not receive as a child. Parenting today is much more challenging than when I was a child, and more challenging than when I was parenting my daughter. Due to family mobility, an increased number of females in the workforce and the loss of a strong sense of community, the need to teach character is growing. Character is a trait that everyone can achieve, regardless of background, riches, or wealth; it can be learned and modeled. It's about doing the right things and making the right decisions when others are watching and when others are not watching. It's self accountability, knowing deep down within that you did your part, the right thing, or the best you could. It is shown by a stranger that helps out in a car accident, a hero who risks his own life to save a child from a burning building; or a colleague who comes to the defense of a person that is being belittled. It's giving the best we have, it's being the best we can be, it's increasing your quality of life by increasing others quality of life.

Learning theories and concepts relative to character is as important as reading, writing, and math and should be taught, modeled, and reinforced first by parents, then by others, including schools, churches, and community organizations.

It is especially important in today's society when there are so many alluring influences, including technology, music, and other forces which challenge children's daily decision making. The growing need for parents to facilitate the modeling and teaching character concepts and a personal need to honestly explore my childhood has inspired me to write this book.

DEDICATION

I dedicate this book to my mother, who had many of her dreams denied, and destroyed. However, through parenting she managed to ensure that the dreams of her nine children were encouraged, and eventually achieved. I am blessed to have her as a mother, and grateful to have benefited from her life struggles. She took advantage of every teachable moment to encourage me and my siblings to set goals and make sound decisions. I salute my mother for her honesty, integrity, her goal setting abilities, ethics, and her teachings.

ACKNOWLEDGEMENTS

I would like to thank my loving family for their support and assistance in this book, more specifically Gary, my husband, for believing in me; Jacques, my daughter, for being an outstanding teacher and making us proud parents, and for assisting with activities for young children, Terrence, my son-in law, for his patience with Jacques when she was assisting me; and my granddaughter, Terriaje', for all the joy she brings while making me aware of the new challenges for parenting and the need to start character education at an early age. I would like to also thank other talented individuals and colleagues assisting with the production of this book:

Dr. Thelma Feaster, who like me sought to discover why some individuals easily put the organizational needs before their own personal needs. The interest in finding an answer to this question sent me back to my childhood for answers; and Mrs. Travella Free, for providing assistance in literature reviews and designing experiential activities. Additionally, I would like to thank Dr. Barbara Marshall and Mrs. Vivian Smith for editing this book as parents, trustworthy individuals, and professionals that are interested in the growth and development of youth. I am grateful for my twelve angels that God blessed me with to give me strength and encouragement to continue helping and inspiring others. Special thanks and appreciation goes to Rev. Dorise Bonds for her heartfelt prayers, genuine support and sincere encouragement; Mrs. Larree Cherry, my integrity role model, for unselfishly sharing her knowledge, and her commitment to excellence; Mrs. Linda McCain and Mrs. Denise Humphrey, professional colleagues, for their trust in me as a person and belief in me as a professional; Dr. Wilda Wade, Mrs. Elaine Morehead-Hughes, Mrs. Linda Thomas, and Mrs. Lena Watson for being good friends for over a decade, who constantly reminds me to slow down, breathe, and take time for myself; Dr. Donald McDowell for being the big brother I was not born with-for supporting, caring, and listening to my career concerns, issues, and dreams; Mrs. Martha Battle, my favorite aunt, who has a heart of gold and a strong belief in family unity, support and caring; and Rev. Jeremiah Battle, my favorite uncle, who lives the word that he so elegantly preaches; who are and has always been my biggest cheerleaders. And my twelfth angel is my sister, Lorita, who remains strong even through her battle with multiple sclerosis, which keeps our family in prayer.

TABLE OF CONTENTS

Preface
Dedication
Acknowledgements
Introduction: Why Exploring "Sensational Me"

1. Understanding Self: A trip back to Childhood 1
   Our Childhood: Stepping Back to Move Forward 7
   Parent Character Check-Up 31

2. Understanding the 5-to-8 Year 35
   Developmental Theory: Children Ages 5-to-8 35
   Teaching Themes 36
   The Social, Mental, Physical, and
     Emotional Characteristics, and Parenting
     Implications for Children Ages 5-to-8 37

3. Creating a Learning Environment at Home 45
   Recommended Educational Activities for
     Children 5-to-8 48
   Using the Experiential Learning Model to
     Teach Critical Thinking 51

Recognizing and Encouraging Young Children	53
Standards for Recognition	53
Individual Recognition	56
Group Recognition	57
Enhancing Character Development while Showing Children Love	58

4. **Experientially Enhancing Character**   61

Activities for 7 and 8 Year Olds	
Building Blocks to Honesty	64
Writing about Honesty	66
Printing for Respect	67
Tracing Respectful Actions	68
My Favorite Chores	69
Responsible Behavior Traits	72
Dressing with Uniqueness	73
Spelling Character Words	74
Helping and Practicing Responsible Behaviors	75
Scrambling to Trustworthiness	78
Family Celebrations and Traditions	78
Things Good Citizen Do	80
Responsibly Handling Emotions	81
Writing Ways to Not Handle Emotions	83
Bag up Anger	83
Handling Anger Feelings	85
Child/Parent Activities	86
Activities for 5 & 6 Year Olds	
We're Different, We're Alike	87
Places to Learn About Others	89
Respecting Diversity	90
Things That Creates Diversity	92
Exploring Other Cultures	93
Characteristics of Cultures	95
Using Good Manners to Show Respect	95
Caring Actions to Show Respect	98

Complimentary Caring Table	98
Sharing Complimentary Actions	100
Caring for Friends	101
Activities Friends Enjoy	104
Responsibly Handling Bullying	105
Responsible Actions	107
Confidently Setting Goals	108
Building Confidence	110
Child/Parent Activities	110
Character Words Defined	113

INTRODUCTION

Why Exploring "Sensational Me"

This book is designed for parents to help them understand themselves and move purposefully through their present life stage of development. It will also help parents understand their 5-to-8 year old, strengthen communications through an enhanced learning atmosphere at home while assisting children to develop character using creative hands-on activities. It is imperative to help children develop character as early as possible. Parents need to take an active role in assisting their children in character development, because children who gain knowledge and skills related to emotional intelligence can easily establish a loving, respectful, and caring relationship with themselves, and others. They tend to be better prepared for the future, and will be better citizens. They are more likely to be successful in life as employees, employers, and long term relationship partners.

Some individuals consider parenting easy but I found parenting to be very difficult. I think it could have been easier if I had a guide or written procedure to follow which allowed me to check and see when I was on track. I needed a scale or readily accessible measurement tool to help determine how I was doing or some way for checks and balances. It was very difficult to find the time to visit the library to acquire books or find experienced adults with the time to assist and advise when I needed it most. Maybe I was too stressed to just go with the flow and really relax. If I were a young mother now, rather than in the middle adulthood life stage of development, parenting would be easier because I have acquired numerous skills, abilities and experiences in designing effective educational programming for children and acquired greater wisdom in a variety of subjects. Most parents of the 5-to-8 year old are young adults in the 20 something age group. I remember when I was in my twenties; I just wanted a good night's sleep, the resources to pay all the monthly bills, a little understanding and support from my husband, and relief from multitasking. Parenting is one very important job that we have among numerous other jobs and things that we are required to do. Unfortunately, there is no financial gain or monetary pay, no annual evaluations, no checkups, no required parent training, nor annual salary increases. If we are not good parents we may not know it immediately. If we are good parents we may or may not be rewarded by successful, financially secure, responsible children maturing into competent adults. Most parents really do a good job and are comforted by the fact that they do the best they can with the resources and skills that they have at the time.

Some view parenting as an opportunity to give children all the things they wanted and missed in their own childhood, or as an opportunity to live a second childhood. Oftentimes there is an inner conflict relative to experiencing a second childhood. As a parent, you want to give your child all the things you wanted as a child versus doing what you know is right and best for their development. It is very important for adults to identify and understand their personal truths. Personal truths affect how we parent. Many of our personal truths stem from childhood transitions, challenges, issues, successes, achievements and experiences. I realize that many of the values influencing my life decisions are strongly connected to my childhood desires and needs. Writing this book and journaling required me to take an honest and thorough childhood reflection which helped me to understand my parenting style. I discovered that I have a need to nurture others; I better understand my standard for character and integrity, my strong work ethnic, and my feelings about family and other relationships. Most importantly writing this book has helped me to move to a happier place in life. The reflection to childhood unveiled: unethical people and negative situations I wanted to forget; ethical people with high character; positive situations that I am proud of, which brought smiles to my face; and a wonderful village that contributed to my well-being.

I realize that the experiences and challenges I had as a child has contributed to my ethical standards of excellence and my success as a spouse, parent, grandmother, daughter, aunt, sister, and employee in a position that affords me an opportunity to help others. After I discovered so much about myself, I included self-discovery as the first chapter in this book. I believe that parenting starts with adults, knowing, understanding, respecting and valuing self. As a parent, I have found that I need to continuously review and update my knowledge of self, just as I have done as related to my career. As a result of updating my needs on a regular basis every five years, I have found that needs and values changed as they were satisfied, goals were taken to a higher level as goals were accomplished, and interests and standards were modified as I prepare for retirement. The personal needs and interests of parents directly affect their preferred parenting style.

There are four chapters in this book. The first chapter takes the reader on a trip back to childhood to reflect on childhood experiences. It also helps the reader look at self by reflecting on their childhood and the relationship of one's childhood to adult parenting styles. The second chapter helps parents understand the characteristics of the 5-to-8 year old and identifies appropriate learning theories for use with the 5-to-8 year old in individual and group settings. The third chapter gives ideals and considerations for creating a learning atmosphere at home, experiential learning model and involves the parents in a discussion on recognizing, praising and encouraging children. The fourth chapter focuses on experiential activities that promote critical thinking to enhance character development. The goal of this chapter is to equip parents with strategies to take an active role in teaching and enforcing character development at home through effective modeling and purposeful learning experiences and activities. More specifically, this book is designed to:

- Help parents understand self

- Increase parental understanding of young children and how they learn

- Enhance the home learning environment

- Strengthen parent/child communications

- Experientially teach Character concepts

CHAPTER 1

Understanding Self: A trip back to Childhood

There are numerous human developmental theorists, I prefer the teachings of Robert Havighurst, who in 1987, stressed the importance of mastering developmental tasks appropriate to a given life stage before moving to the next stage. Developmental psychology explores the changes that occur throughout one's life-span — from year to year, month to month, and even day to day. It involves the scientific study of the growth, development, and behavioral changes in humans from conception through old age. The theories emanating from developmental psychology illustrate patterns of growth and change. These theories also shed light on how these changes affect parenting. This knowledge increases effectiveness in anticipating and planning strategies to live harmoniously and address life transitions.

A cycle of growth and change can be predicted. This cycle is characterized as a process of biological, social, and psychological events. By understanding the normal stresses and changes of each period of life, one is less likely to be overwhelmed by them. As we pass through stages in our development, we develop specific skills and physical capabilities appropriate to our age. Understanding one's physical, emotional, cognitive, and social stages helps us form realistic developmental expectations. Likewise, sensitivity to the developmental life stage of others will assist parents in managing their day to day experiences and life transitions.

For children ages 5-to-8, the average age of parents is 25 to 35. The life stage of this group is early adulthood, which involves the developmental tasks of marriage, childbearing, work, and lifestyle. During early adulthood, adults establish a lifestyle that will serve as a framework for the rest of adulthood. This lifestyle includes a balance between work and leisure, establishing friendships at varying levels of intimacy and the selection of activities that reflect value orientation.

The most important factors contributing to lifestyle are marriage partners, children, and careers. Also during early adulthood, the world view broadens, and appreciations of the interdependence of systems develop. One of the major sources of stress in this life stage is the struggle to balance roles. Early adulthood is difficult because of the number of tasks to be performed, the lack of experience, and inadequate skills. During this stage, necessary tasks are all competing for time. There just does not seem to be enough time to manage all of life's obligations. Often, it is necessary to multitask, performing three of more tasks at once, which can be frustrating and overwhelming at times.

Over the past few years, there has been a significant increase in the number of grandparents raising children. This is due to a variety of reasons including the inability of parents to care for their children because of physical or medical conditions, substance abuse, military duty, or other reasons. This responsibility interrupts the normal developmental stage for grandparents because caring for children is very demanding and challenging. When grandparents are caring for grandchildren, oftentimes their needs and care is neglected because there is not time or energy to efficiently address both sets of needs.

As a person in the middle adulthood life stage, I find that it takes more energy than I want to expel when caring for my grandchild. I find myself needing to plan other activities and responsibilities around our visit. When the visit is over, I am very happy for our time together, but usually exhausted. One challenge for parents in the middle and later adulthood stage is the declining ability to move really fast and multitask effectively. Lots of parents in this age group prefer to do one thing at the time. A good understanding of these stages helps adults plan better and understand the importance of effective time management. Havighurst grouped the **developmental tasks** for adults into the following three groups.

Young Adulthood (18 to 30)
    a. Selecting a marriage partner
    b. Adjusting to, and living with a marriage partner
    c. Starting a family and accepting the new role of parent
    d. Learning to manage household responsibilities
    e. Starting a career and continuing one's education
    f. Assuming civic responsibility/voluntarism
    g. Searching for a congenial social group

Middle Adulthood (30 to 60)
    a. Assisting teenage children in becoming responsible, coping, and caring adults
    b. Nurturing the marital relationship
    c. Developing leisure & volunteer activities
    d. Management of household
    e. Management of Career
    f. Adjusting to aging parents
    g. Accepting and adjusting to the physiological changes of life

CREATIVELY EXPLORING

Late Adulthood (60 to the end of life)
   a. Establishing a connection with one's age group
   a. Redirecting energy toward new roles/retirement and reduced income
   b. Accepting one's life and adapting to changing social roles
   c. Developing a point of view about death
   d. Establishing satisfactory physical living arrangements
   e. Adjusting to decreasing health and physical strength

In addition to developmental stages, we are products of our experiences, how we parent will be affected by our childhood, the things we desire to protect our children from, the things that we have experienced, whether good or bad, personal and family values, family celebrations, how our family functioned, and how we felt as a part of our family growing up. Because our childhood is very significant to our adulthood and our parenting style and preferences, this chapter is devoted to looking back on our childhood. It's important to take the time to reflect and journal in order to identify and deal with past negative and positive experiences and then decide how to use experiences to enhance our present and future lives which may affect the growth and development of our children.

When I first started the literature research for this book, social behaviorists said that it is important to understand your own childhood by answering certain questions including:
- the things you remember enjoying doing with family
- the things that siblings did together
- things that enhanced your sense of community

I think a the following items are very important and should also be included:
- volunteer activities
- ethical people

DR. SHIRLEY B. MCNEILL

- unethical people
- birth order
- parents' parenting style
- memorable events

Thinking back to childhood, I found it very difficult to recall the fun and enjoyable things. I remember the importance of church, friends, family, school, and my neighbors.

As I kept thinking harder, I could remember a few things that were related to me being my brothers and sisters "hero" like making my brothers, sisters and parents pajamas for Christmas, my brother asking me to make him a pair of shoes, or my older brother always trying to follow me to the movies, or to my friends house. But the thing I remember most were the sacrifices and caring I gave to my siblings to increase their quality of life. I also remembered a few negative actions of unethical people that I didn't want to remember. There have been pivotal events, people, and things that bring joy and are wonderful and there may also be events so painful that we unconsciously seek to forget them. I now realize that it is important to remember these events, people and situations because they definitely affect how we view things and situations. In order to move pass them and grow from the experiences, we must first identify them, and then deal with them where necessary and accept our real responsibility for them. The more I reflected, the more important the memories became to my journey. I found this to be a useful experience in helping me to identify and understand my parenting preferences and style, needs and interests, ethics, character development, decision-making challenges, and how I journeyed to my present, wonderfully peaceful place in life.

Before we can raise children with character, we must check and be aware or our own character development through

CREATIVELY EXPLORING

experiences. It's important to know and understand your needs, values, ethics, strengths, attitudes, uniqueness, and character development to make sure you are teaching your children the things you want them to learn. Parents are their children's first and most important teachers. Children are like sponges, they act the way we act, they do what we do, they eat what we eat, they respond to issues the way we respond, and they value what we value. They believe what we believe about society, about others, about themselves-their habits are replicas of our habits. We are their role model; we teach when are teaching and trying to make a point-this may occur while standing in line at the food store, or riding in the car, or as a part of the family group, during mealtime, at playtime, or a special setting for learning at home. But we are also teaching when we are not planning to teach-when we don't want to be influencing, when we are not at our best, when we wish they didn't see us, when we make poor decisions, when we say things we wish we hadn't said, when we are angry, when we are having a really bad day, or when we feel bad and act accordingly. As a parent you are **"teaching when you want to teach, and you are teaching when you do not want to teach"**. Children learn by what is modeled by parents and other significant adults. Children will do what you do and not what you tell them to do.

This chapter gives you an opportunity to take time to focus on yourself while going back to your childhood and journaling to identify ethics, decision-making, character development, real needs, and desires that may impact your parenting style. In the next section, "Stepping Back to Move Forward", I shared some of my childhood joys, thoughts, feelings, and situations to stimulate the thought process for you. I found it exhilarating and cleansing to record my experiences. Your honest responses to each question will probably do the same for you and start you on your journey.

DR. SHIRLEY B. MCNEILL

Your Childhood: Stepping Back to Move Forward

As a child, I liked the strong sense of family, community, and **citizenship** in our small town. Members in the community helped each other with babysitting, dealing with life transitions-sickness, death, long work shifts, and other needs. We had homeless people, but we didn't call them homeless, we called them people down on their luck. My parents fed them and gave them clothes. All adults in the community took a personal and serious responsibility for all children in the community. The community served as a village to help all members survive and excel in school, home, church, and society. After entering junior high school, I joined a community action group that visited Assisted Living Homes to assist older adults in crafts and making pot holders. The two hours twice a week that I volunteered was time well spent. I learned at an early age that community service which promotes citizenship was important and the deeds that were done not only helped the recipients but also provided the doer with a huge sense of helping others and giving to society. As a child I wasn't always happy about all the things that were expected of me when I really wanted to go outside and play or just spend time with friends. However, I enjoyed the community spirit and the satisfaction of caring, sharing, and giving that comes with serving others.

1. Write about your childhood joys and your family, community and citizenship:

_____
_____
_____
_____
_____
_____

CREATIVELY EXPLORING

_____
_____
_____
_____
_____
_____
_____

I remember several childhood challenges that enhanced my level of **tolerance** on a day to day basis. Some of the challenges included: lifting heavy clothes to take them in and out of the car, then to the laundry to wash them; taking care of my brothers and sisters when I really wanted to roller skate outside; having to take speech classes in elementary school, because I stuttered; sharing a bed with three other sisters; and enduring the elements while walking to school in the rain, snow, sleet, and cold weather. I also remember falling asleep on the porch and dropping my brother to the porch from my lap, and how bad I felt. Riding the city bus and walking were the most frequent forms of transportation, though we had a car, my step dad worked long hours and was not available to drive us to the laundry, food store, nor other places. My mother did not drive. We were very inconvenienced and spent a lot of time waiting for the bus, walking in bad weather, and waiting for a ride to get from one place to another. Lack of transportation as a child instilled an adult value and need for dependable and safe means of transportation to the extent of needing to own at least two cars that are always serviced and road ready.

2. Write about activities and events that challenged you and enhanced your tolerance, try to remember how it made you feel.

_____
_____
_____
_____

DR. SHIRLEY B. MCNEILL

_____
_____
_____
_____
_____

My great aunt, who was more like my grandmother, was a lady with **integrity**. She was consistent in her actions, courteous to others, and loyal to family, friends, and her church. Every March she made me a birthday cake, on the weekend she braided my hair, and wrapped my hair to make it stylish. She didn't have a lot of money, so she purchased clothes for me from the thrifty market-a used clothing store-she would say it is not new, but it's new to you. She was honest, reliable and loved me, she took me to church–I went by her house everyday after school and on Saturdays and Sundays. Most days we would swing in her large wooden swing on the front porch and talk about school, church, and sewing. I felt special and happy when I was with her.

3. Other than your parents, who were the important people of integrity in your young childhood?

_____
_____
_____
_____
_____
_____
_____
_____
_____

CREATIVELY EXPLORING

_____
_____
_____
_____
_____

My great uncle, who was married to my aunt and actually my blood relative, as best as I can recall, was an unethical person who was **not** respectful, considerate of others feelings, kind, caring, fair, nor trustworthy. He was a really mean and abusive man–he shouted at my great aunt and I. He was verbally abrasive, threatened us, called me a boy, used disparaging terms towards me and demanded that Aunt Gertrude attend to his needs including fixing his plate of food. She had to stop what she was doing and wait on him. He used to take us to the store and other places, but he did not want us to talk, he threatened to put us out of his pick-up truck if we didn't stop talking. He made my great aunt and I feel insignificant, unloved, and not valued. Spending time in my uncle's company made me sad, but being with my aunt made me very happy. I guess I just took the bad with the good.

4. Write about persons who affected your quality of life due to lack of good character and people skills.

_____
_____
_____
_____
_____
_____
_____
_____

DR. SHIRLEY B. MCNEILL

I now realize that there were actions from people from my childhood that I could not control, but there is a need to deal with how their actions impacted my life and challenged my **character** and **integrity**. I had forgotten the things I would like to forget, it has taken me nearly four months to remember the negatives from my childhood. It was very difficult for me to remember that I did not grow teeth until age five and my uncles were constantly laughing and talking about my lack of teeth, they would give me foods that were difficult to eat without teeth then laugh at my persistence to eat the foods. I remember the summer I went on the trip with the church, I was sitting on the side of the pool, someone came up behind me and pushed me in the water, I nearly drowned. It has taken a long time to get over my fear of water.

There were three situations involving unethical men, the first happened numerous times while I was babysitting, the neighbor would come home, then stand in a place where only I could see him, then he would touch his genitals, the second incident happened while I was cleaning a neighbor's house for pay and the husband offered me a dollar and candy to touch my breast. The third incident was a stranger who was a prominent businessman owning a department store where I had applied

CREATIVELY EXPLORING

for a job. He got my address from the application and came to my house and told me he had a job for me, but the job was not in the department store, the job was taking care of him.

Additionally, I dealt with inequalities due to a blended family, and observing a shooting that ended in death. This took place in front of my house while I sat on the front porch. Through all of these situations I made good, responsible decisions even though these experiences caused me to feel unworthy, ashamed, shocked and disgusted as a pre-teen and teen.

5. List three to five of the most defining experiences in your childhood or things you would like to forget, that challenged your **integrity** and **character**.

_____
_____
_____
_____
_____
_____
_____
_____
_____
_____
_____
_____

Starting very early in life I learned about work, I had chores after school. After I finished my chores, I did my brother's chores to make sure he didn't get a whipping. He got one whipping for not doing his chores; I think his whipping affected me more than it did him. If he did not do his chores, I did his chores to ensure that he did not get another whipping. I never wanted to have to hear him cry and scream from the pain of the whipping. His whipping was bad because our dad disciplined my brothers. My self-sacrificing started early in life, probably with this incident. As I got older, I worked after school and during the summers. I learned very early about saving, planning, budgeting, and managing **money**. There was little pay for hard work and a little money went a long way when I was a child. There was very little money for toys, and meals away from home. I learned how to save and manage money not from allowances, but from the money I earned working after school. The respect and value for money as a child shaped me into a frugal money manager as an adult. We had a strong **work ethic** and believed in hard work. Arriving on time, meeting work goals, and practicing responsible behaviors and **accountability** were the expected norms. My strong work ethic established as a child has carried over to adulthood and influences my standard of excellence and persistence in the workplace.

We valued **education,** worked hard, and persistently in school and viewed education as a way to achieve a higher quality of life. Throughout my life I have never forgotten the constant lecturing received from my mother, telling me how important it was to get an education and be independent, not having to ask anyone for money to pay for life's necessities. My belief in education and its value was an inner force and need that pushed me to acquire a Ph.D. We respected and valued all **older adults** and addressed them with the highest level of respect, always referring to them with Mr. or Mrs. in front of their names. Our grandparents played a very significant role in our lives and usually had the last word in major family decisions. In fact, I conducted extensive research and wrote my first book on Older Adults Volunteerism as a part of my doctoral dissertation. We were **religious,** and went to church every

CREATIVELY EXPLORING

Sunday and were active in church related events and activities. This tradition of being in touch with spirituality still exists in my family and is as strong as ever.

6. Discuss core **values** you learned in childhood and how your family viewed such things as money, education, work ethics, older adults, religion, and citizenship/volunteerism.

Money:_____
_____
_____
_____
_____
_____
_____
_____

Education:_____
_____
_____
_____
_____
_____

Work Ethics/Accountability: _____
_____
_____
_____
_____
_____
_____
_____
_____
_____

DR. SHIRLEY B. MCNEILL

OlderAdults:

Religion/Tolerance/Acceptance:

Citizenship:

CREATIVELY EXPLORING

Others:_____
_____
_____
_____
_____
_____
_____
_____
_____
_____
_____
_____

As a child growing up in the 50's and 60's our family operated on the belief that men ruled and were highly **respected**, they earned most of the money and made all the decisions about meals, furniture, family clothing, and housing. Our family had two incomes; however, my mother's salary was considerably less than my stepfather. Men were not expected to help with the management and operation of the home, nor parenting. They did not go to church, PTA or other family oriented activities. I never remember my parents taking a vacation or doing fun activities together. By my parents' actions, I was taught that men and boys were respected and if women didn't like the actions of men they had to suffer in silence because **anger** was not a feeling to be expressed by females. I learned to smile when I was angry and suffered in silence because women did not get angry. I never saw my mother express anger, but once, I can't remember what I had done, but I remember having to go to the fence in the backyard to get the switch and then I got a whipping with it. Not learning how to express and manage anger as a child proved to be a skill that needed to be learned as an adult. I am sure that this inability relative to expressing and managing anger contributed to the demise of some of my important relationships. I have painfully learned that anger is normal and need to be dealt with quickly and constructively. However, my lifestyle and relationship has improved and is a two income household where salaries are nearly equal and decisions are jointly made about meals, clothing, and housing. My husband is expected and helps with the management and operation of our household and we have mutual respect and attend church, plan, and take vacations as a family. Family communications and joint decision making is effective and satisfying and I have learned to peacefully deal with anger.

7. List four family expectations, beliefs, or attitudes which were acceptable in your childhood, which are neither acceptable nor useful to your lifestyle today.

Family Beliefs/Attitudes:_____
_____
_____
_____
_____
_____
_____
_____
_____
_____
_____
_____
_____
_____
_____

I definitely wanted my child to experience the extended family where grandparents, aunts, uncles and cousins were

CREATIVELY EXPLORING

one to two blocks away and the sense of community where neighbors pitched in and assisted each other-whether it was giving trusted advice in time of relational crisis or personal problems or assistance in child care when it was necessary to work late. I also wanted my child to experience the joy and sense of accomplishment gained from helping others learn new skills. When I was in the ninth grade, I remember volunteering at the community center after school; two days a week to assist older adults develop sewing skills. When the ladies see me around town they called me the sewing lady and expressed their appreciation for my assistance. I learned at an early age that community service was important and satisfied my need to help others. As an adult, I still enjoy helping others and I believe that helping others through training by teaching and inspiring is my true purpose in life.

8. What things from your childhood do you want your child to experience?

_____
_____
_____
_____
_____
_____
_____
_____
_____
_____
_____
_____
_____

I wanted to protect my child from having too much responsibility; I wanted her to have time and freedom to be a child –to play outside, to spend more time at the park in free play and to experience more conveniences in life, such as family transportation, and regular allowances. I wanted her to have a bedroom just for her to experience her own personal space to be responsible for, to decorate, and to express herself. Additionally, I wanted to protect her from people who are not trustworthy, considerate, self-disciplined, good citizens, responsible, and honest or anyone who would not increase her quality of life. Our social support included a few families from our neighborhood and church. We participated in many activities as a family unit with no occasions where Jacques was alone with an adult other than in school or church. And finally, I wanted to protect her from a near drowning and the fear of water by learning to swim at an early age.

9. What things from your childhood do you want to protect your child from experiencing?

CREATIVELY EXPLORING

In an effort to protect my daughter from too much **responsibility**, and provide a higher level of living, I overprotected, provided her with many luxuries, and did not provide enough real opportunities for her to earn privileges, money, and experiences. Like many children from two income families, I received little quality communications and personal one-on-one interactions from my parents. Communications was mostly instructions on what needed to be done, checks to make sure things were done, or appointing me to assist other families that needed help. I now realize that responsibility and involvement in the community through opportunities to help others are the things that promoted and encouraged my **integrity** and **ethics** at a very young age. Because I did not provide as many opportunities for my daughter to become involved in the community and accept responsibility for all of her actions at a young age, it took her longer to become financially secure, make **sound decisions**, and decide on a career. Protecting my daughter from my childhood experiences did her give a strong sense of family with honest and regular communications, a sense of flexibility in free time, and a stronger and **confident** sense of self.

10. If you felt a need to protect your child from something or someone, What did your protection of childhood experiences really contribute to your child's development of character?

_____
_____
_____
_____
_____
_____
_____
_____

DR. SHIRLEY B. MCNEILL

As the oldest of nine, I was the typical first born, conservative, reliable, wanting to please, conscientious, a good student and worker, patient, and tolerant. I did and still have a need for approval, but will go on and get things done without it. My sister that was next to me was the total opposite of me, she was strong willed, aggressive and the disciplinarian. My sisters and brothers who were middle born were quiet, friendly, outgoing, competitive, peacemakers, easygoing, and manipulators depending on the situations at different times and whether they were boys or girls. The girls tended to be more outgoing, friendly, and manipulators while the boys were more competitive, easygoing, and peacemakers. My baby brother and sister, our family's last born, were outgoing, charming, affectionate, spoiled, carefree, a little rebellious, and broke all the rules. My daughter was an only child who tended to be a lot like most first born, but she also tended to be critical, spoiled, affectionate, charming, and outgoing.

11. Use a check to denote your parents, a favorite sibling, and your birth order.

	Mother	Father	Sibling	Yours
Oldest Child				
Only Child				
Middle Child				
Baby Child				

Most of the time, my daughter was a lot like me-a very nurturing, encouraging, and loving person. However, I realized that I was teaching when I was not at my best and didn't want to teach when my daughter started driving. In the driver's seat, she became a different person, she was impatient, rude, inconsiderate, and in a huge hurry. It was shocking at first to see her driving style. Then, I realized her driving style and actions were very similar, okay her driving

CREATIVELY EXPLORING

style and actions were just like mine. At that point, when I saw myself how others see me, I slowly modified my driving attitude and style and accepted the fact that we are teaching when we are teaching and we are teaching when we are not intending to teach!

12. Think back, record a parenting situation when you were teaching when you did not intend to teach.

_____
_____
_____
_____
_____
_____
_____
_____
_____
_____
_____
_____
_____
_____
_____
_____

In looking at temperament let's define the terms used in the scale. Regularity denotes the irregular or regular pattern of physical functions and activities such as eating and sleeping. Mood refers to the positive or negative communications and behaviors. Withdrawal and cooperate defines how one respond to new situations, changes in schedule, or transitions. Intensity is the energy level one exerts. Attention span relates to the interest and length of time one usually stay with a task. Adaptability refers to the ease or difficulty in adjusting to new situations.

13. Using the words adequate or inadequate, rate your parent's, an older sibling, and your temperament on the variables below.

                            Mother Father Sibling(oldest) Yours

Regularity:
Mood:
Withdrawal or Cooperate:
Intensity:
Attention Span:
Adaptability:

Learning styles defines our most effective way to learn. There are three main learning styles, including auditory-learning is best by hearing the task explained; visual learners need to see the task done and kinesthetic learners are interested in actually doing the task, they are hands-on.

14. Using a check, mark the learning style of your parents, your youngest sister or brother, and yours.

               Mother   Father   Sibling Yours
                                                      (youngest)

Auditory
Visual
Kinesthetic

Most parents use a combination of parenting styles depending on the situation, I can remember times when my parents used all three styles. The parent who uses the authoritarian parenting style is interested in maintaining control. Parents who use the permissive parenting style establishes no limits, expectations, structure, nor rules, while a parent who uses the respectful parenting style is interested in mutual communications. Most of the time my mother used the permissive parenting style with me. I was a child with high character, making good responsible decisions was expected and required. It was always important to me to not let anyone down, help all the people that needed helping, take care of my younger brothers and sisters, and to be trustworthy by not disappointing my mother. I appreciated the goodness and kindness bestowed on me by my aunt, grandmother, and teachers. I think that deep down I thought I needed to earn love, trust, kindness, respect, and caring. My parents praised and encouraged my caring, assistance, and helpfulness to others and depended on me to assist when and where needed. The fact that I received praise for performance as a child has carried over to adulthood making performance at work and home an important standard to measure achievement. I am most comfortable and happy when I am busy, even when I need to take a time out and do nothing.

15. What things did your parent do to make their parenting style effective?

_____
_____
_____
_____
_____
_____
_____
_____
_____
_____
_____
_____
_____
_____
_____
_____
_____

I wish I could have had more time with my parents, a time just for me, a time to learn how to set boundaries, and learn more about self-nurturing. I wish I had learned that anger is normal and how to peacefully deal with it. I learned selflessness because there were so many people in need and I was a caring, empathizing, and a considerate person even as a child. Most of all, **I wish I had learned how to give and show love, respect, nurturing, and value myself when I was very young. Having these skills would have significantly enhanced my quality of life.** I did learn how to love, respect, and value myself after my separation and divorce. For the first time in life, in my late 40's, I took the time to focus on my needs, establish boundaries, define relational absolutes and identify my uniqueness. I did like so many others; I lost myself in marriage, work, and parenting.

16. What things do you wish you had received when you were a child?

CREATIVELY EXPLORING

As the oldest of nine, I experienced a great deal of responsibility in caring for my younger brothers and sisters. I did not receive enough nurturing. As a teen, I did not date, but I was allowed to go to the movies on Sundays with a girl friend. Since I did not date, I did not learn how to relate in male/female relationships, establish boundaries, and establish a comfort level in relational negotiations. I wanted my daughter to experience dating, memberships in social clubs with others her age, participation in events and activities after school, and other relational experiences. Additionally, I wanted her to have open communications with lots of one- on- one time with me to ensure enough time to discuss issues, concerns, and peer pressures. I used respectful parenting styles most of the time and sometimes permissive. My parenting style was not always effective because my daughter was very opinionated, stubborn, and confident sometimes, then just the opposite at other times. There were times when she needed the authoritarian parenting style. Jacques' dad used the authoritarian style and was respected, and valued as a parent. I was respected and valued as a friend first and as a parent second. As a parent, I thought at the time my parenting sometimes was effective but I now realize that I gave what I wanted to receive as a child which was not always what my child needed.

17. Identify the effect your childhood had on your parenting style.

_____
_____
_____
_____
_____
_____
_____
_____
_____

DR. SHIRLEY B. MCNEILL

My family had transportation but it was not enough to support tasks that **needed** to be performed outside the home, weekly activities included trips to the launderette to wash clothes, downtown to pay bills, and the food store to purchase groceries. There was a need for assistance in parenting my brothers and sisters, and more family support from relatives. There were many **strengths,** I remember my mother's ability to manage money, including: stretching a small salary to pay many bills and her wonderful sense of humor-especially when she did not know the answer to problems with school work- she would say funny things to relieve stress. My parents' **joys** included: children making good grades and doing well in school and spending time with friends, helping neighbors and family when in need. We were expected to actively attend and participate in church service and activities, including the junior choir, Sunday School, and church holiday and other special programs.

18. Name two needs, strengths, and joys of your parents that you remember from your childhood.

Needs:_____

CREATIVELY EXPLORING

Strengths: _____
_____
_____
_____
_____
_____
_____

Joys: _____
_____
_____
_____
_____
_____
_____

As a parent my **needs** included making a real contribution to society and a chance to give all that I did not receive as a child to another human being. My parenting **strengths**: includes respect for others, a strong sense of responsibility, genuinely caring attitude toward others, and a strong work ethic. I have acquired a wealth of knowledge and skills in human development; familiarity with best parenting practices research and literature reviews, and exposure to lots of information on strategies for living a harmonious family life. My husband and I were committed to being involved and active in parenting, and supporting school through attending and participating in PTA's, volunteering at school, school fund raisers, and serving as a resource person for school programs. Religion and spiritual well-being through church and church related activities was important. My **joys** were my daughter's happiness, schools success, active participation in cheerleading, extra-curricula activities; good grades; acquiring a BS degree, marriage, childbirth, career as elementary school teacher, obtaining financial security, and good character.

19. Name three needs, strengths, and joys you experienced as a result of parenting.

Needs:_____
_____
_____
_____

Strengths:_____
_____
_____
_____

Joys:_____
_____
_____
_____

20. Without any influence from me, reflect on an event, transition, person, character traits, or an emotional significant experience and write how it impacted your life, parenting, or character.

_____
_____
_____
_____
_____
_____
_____
_____
_____
_____
_____

CREATIVELY EXPLORING

Sometimes our culture's norm, values, beliefs and ways of knowing increase our quality of life as children but with changing times they do not increase our quality of life in today's world. We need to make a conscious effort to redefine our values, beliefs, and ways of knowing and acting to respond to our present needs and style of living. Journaling may help you to notice that as a parent, you are similar or different to your parents on some variables such as joys, needs, strengths, and values. During this experience you may also identify situations where you blamed yourself for others actions that you had no control over. You may recall situations that could have affected you negatively, laws that are not enforced, decisions made at a young age, and events that took place in your environment that were hard to cope with. It is important to remember past events, and then place responsibility for any guilt, shame, anger, fear, or hurt where they should be. It is important to accept any responsibility you should own, forgive those that offended, and learn to truly and fully love and accept yourself as the sensational person you are. When this is done, the rest of your life will be guilt free which will place you in a better position to model and teach character.

DR. SHIRLEY B. MCNEILL

Parent Character Check-Up

Directions: Check yes or no to the following character related sentences. Your responses will assist you in identifying areas that may need your attention.

1. Did I return money to the store when I was given too much change? Yes No

2. Do I volunteer at least one to two hours a week, month, or annually? Yes No

3. Do I use profanity when angered? Yes No

4. Do I accept responsibility for all my actions, even when I felt I had no choice? Yes No

5. If I found a wallet with $10,000 in it, would I return it with all the money in it? Yes No

6. Do I give to a charity? Yes No

7. Have I cheated in a relationship? Yes No

8. Do I use illegal drugs? Yes No

9. Have I told my child to answer the phone and say I am not home, when I am at home? Yes No

10. Do I cheat on my taxes? Yes No

11. Do I stop others from calling a co-worker a negative name? Yes No

CREATIVELY EXPLORING

12. *Do I have the courage to do right, even when others in my presence are corrupt?*   Yes No

13. *Do I honor others' property, and refrain from stealing?*   Yes No

14. *Am I accountable for all my actions?*   Yes No

15. *Do I treat others fairly?*   Yes No

16. *Do I obey the speed limit, and other traffic laws?*   Yes No

17. *Do you treat others fairly regardless of job title?*   Yes No

18. *Do you ask others to perform tasks that you are not willing to perform?*   Yes No

19. *Do you show consideration of others in your acts, words, and deeds?*   Yes No

20. *Do you think you are better than others of a different race, gender, ethnicity, religion, income, age group, or other group?*   Yes No

21. *Do you use the same rules and standards for friends, colleagues, and family as you use for yourself?*   Yes No

22. *Do you value your children, colleagues, spouse, and others enough to listen to them with an open mind?*   Yes No

23. *Do you do your share to make home, work, and your child's school a productive place to work, live, and learn?*   Yes No

24. *Did you express gratitude to a coworker you know did an outstanding job or enhanced the organization through their efforts?*   Yes No

25. *Do you demonstrate to friends and family that you care about them?*   Yes No

26. *Do you demonstrate to colleagues that you care about them?*   Yes No

27. *Do you approach others in a mannerly, polite, kind, and caring way?*   Yes No

28. *Do you demonstrate control of your temper and feelings at work, even if you are the boss?*   Yes No

29. *Do you make it a habit to treat others the way you want to be treated?*   Yes No

30. *Do you think that you are Sensational?*   Yes No

31. *Do you know a Sensational person?*   Yes No

CHAPTER 2

Understanding the 5-to-8 Year Old
Developmental Theory: Children Ages 5-to-8

All children do not develop and grow at the same rate. Nonetheless, they do progress through similar stages of growth at some time in their development. It is helpful for parents to recognize and understand the different developmental stages of children. Familiarity with these stages makes it possible to ensure learning experiences and growth patterns are relevant. Some children may remain at a stage of development longer than others. Some concepts and tasks are more difficult than others for children to achieve, which makes it necessary to understand your child and how they develop in different task areas. On the other hand, a particular activity may be too elementary for a more advanced child. In that case, parents will need to substitute a more advanced experience for the activity in question.

By the time your child is 5 years old, you are very sure of his or her temperament. Temperaments are qualities we are born with but they may be modified in the early years of development. Children are like adults in that they are not the same everyday, but each child has his or her usual adaptability and emotional style. You're probably very aware of your child activity level, their ability to develop a regular pattern for physical functions such as eating and sleeping, the way they respond to new situations, or changes in routine, how adaptable they are, their energy levels, their moods, and attention span. Identifying and knowing your child temperament can make smoother transitions from home to daycare, play and recreation times, learning styles and strategies for cognitive stimulation, and in other daily transitions.

The following **teaching themes** can assist parents in designing developmentally appropriate, hands-on learning experiences and activities for children ages 5-to-8.

- The 5-year-old is interested in health and social studies themes that focus on such routines as bathing, brushing teeth, saying good-night, and going to sleep. These themes connect home, school, and subject matter in a way that the 5-year-old will find irresistible.
- The 6-year-old is interested in exploring the lives of artists and their styles of painting or drawing. They learn primarily through their senses. This theme is tangible and visual, and increases the awareness of the work of great artists.
- The 7-year-old is interested in comparing fairy tales and folk tales from different cultures and eras. This theme broadens children's understanding of different cultures.
- The 8-year-old is interested in a conceptual theme that examines the history of fashion in the 20th century. They are especially interested in looking at changes in clothing, and how clothing is designed, made, and marketed. They are also interested in social issues, such as using animals to make clothes. They have a fascination for how things work.

DR. SHIRLEY B. MCNEILL

Illustrations 1-8: *The Social, Mental, Physical, and Emotional Characteristics, and Parenting Implications for Children Ages 5-to-8*

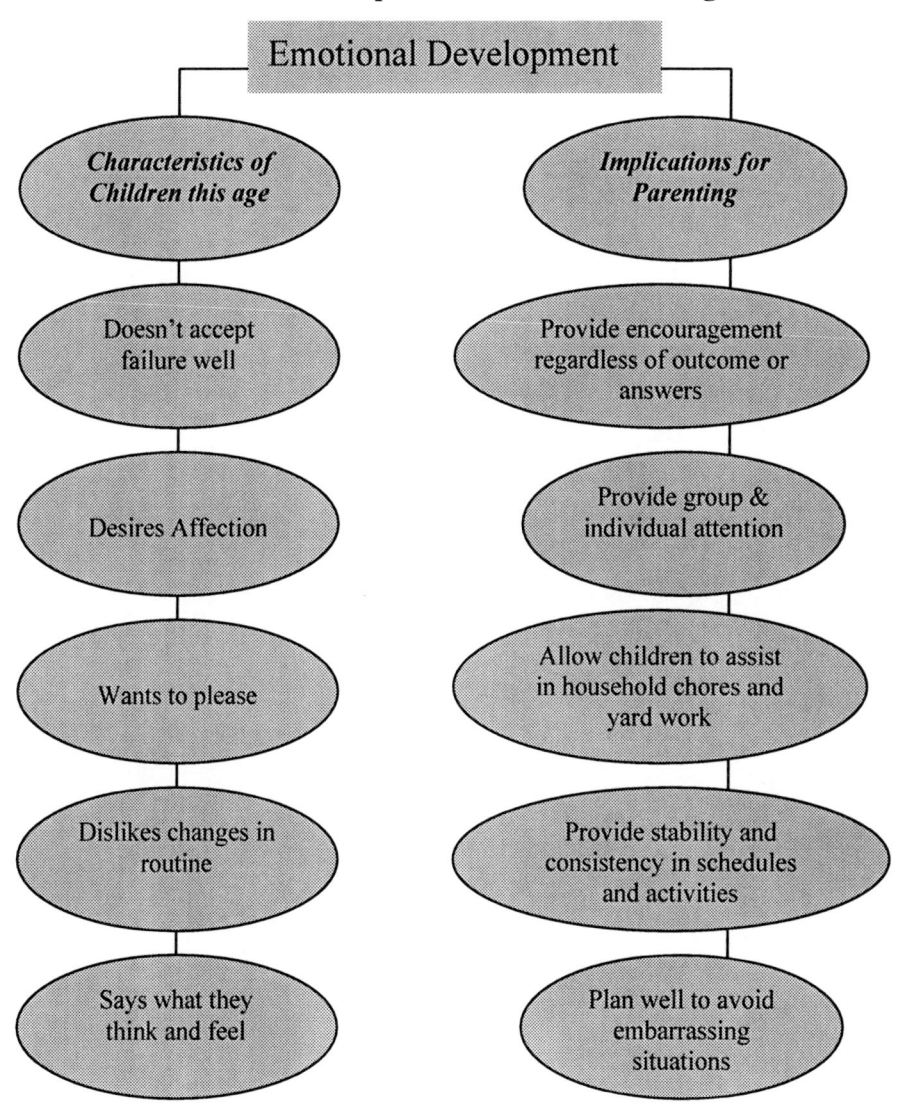

Illustration 1
Characteristics and Implications for Children Ages 5-6

Emotional Development

Characteristics of Children this age	Implications for Parenting
Doesn't accept failure well	Provide encouragement regardless of outcome or answers
Desires Affection	Provide group & individual attention
Wants to please	Allow children to assist in household chores and yard work
Dislikes changes in routine	Provide stability and consistency in schedules and activities
Says what they think and feel	Plan well to avoid embarrassing situations

CREATIVELY EXPLORING

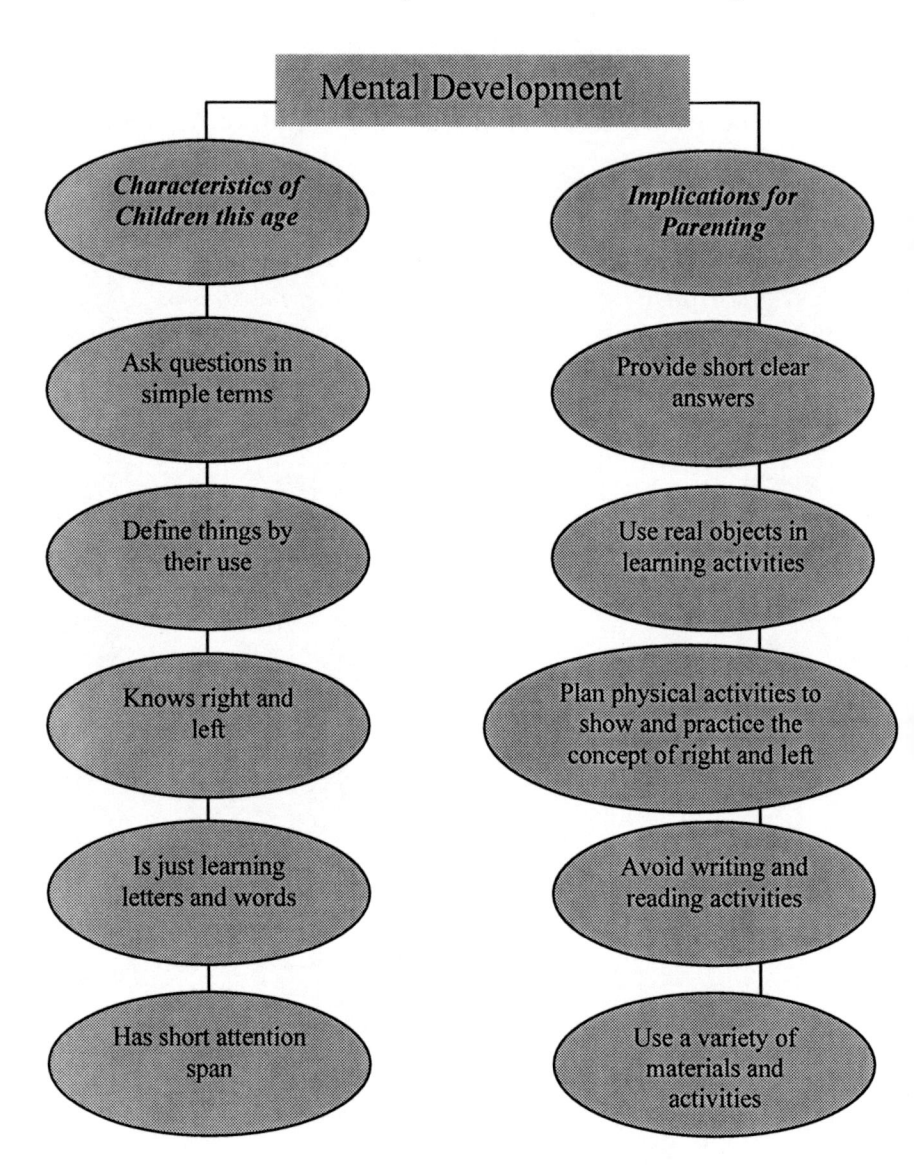

Illustration 2
Characteristics and Implications for Children Ages 5-6

Mental Development

Characteristics of Children this age	*Implications for Parenting*
Ask questions in simple terms	Provide short clear answers
Define things by their use	Use real objects in learning activities
Knows right and left	Plan physical activities to show and practice the concept of right and left
Is just learning letters and words	Avoid writing and reading activities
Has short attention span	Use a variety of materials and activities

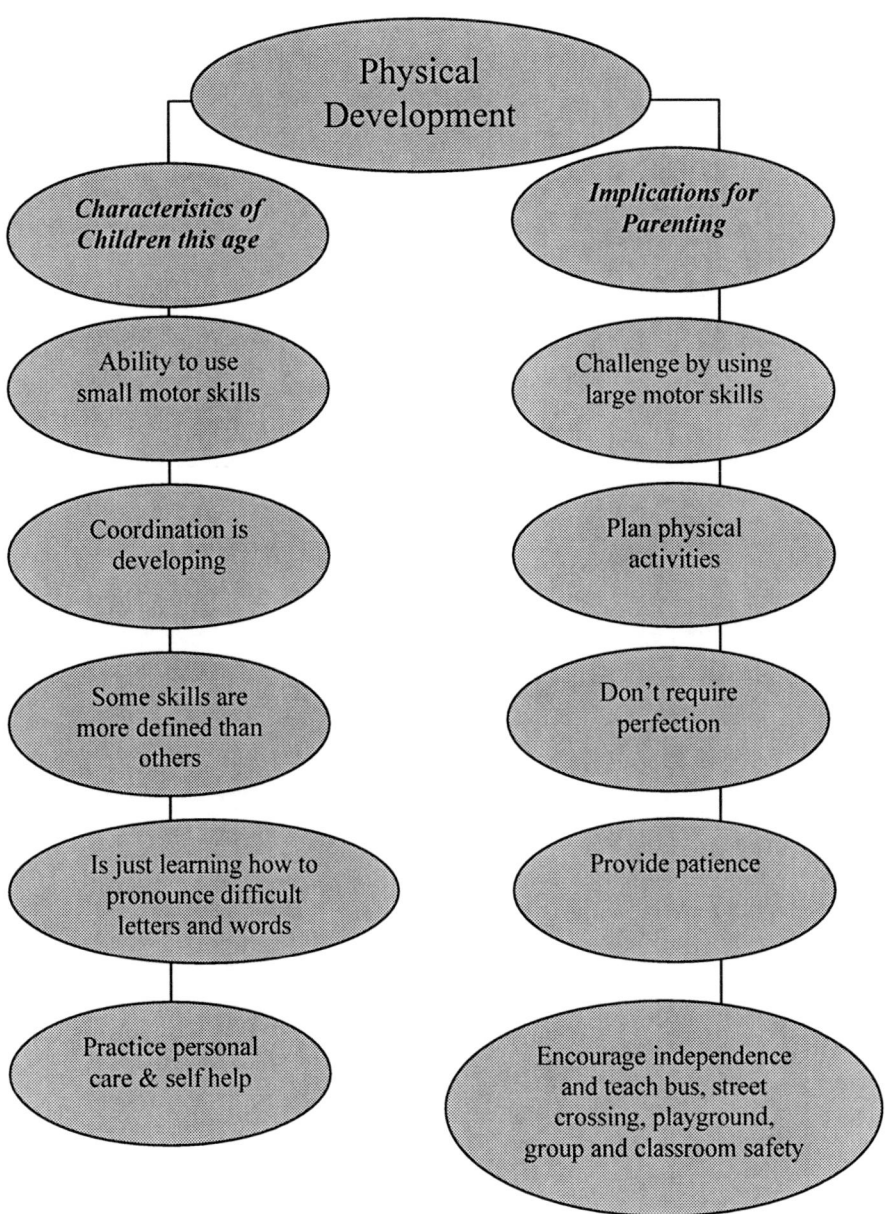

Illustration 3
Characteristics and Implications for Children Ages 5-6

Physical Development

Characteristics of Children this age

- Ability to use small motor skills
- Coordination is developing
- Some skills are more defined than others
- Is just learning how to pronounce difficult letters and words
- Practice personal care & self help

Implications for Parenting

- Challenge by using large motor skills
- Plan physical activities
- Don't require perfection
- Provide patience
- Encourage independence and teach bus, street crossing, playground, group and classroom safety

CREATIVELY EXPLORING

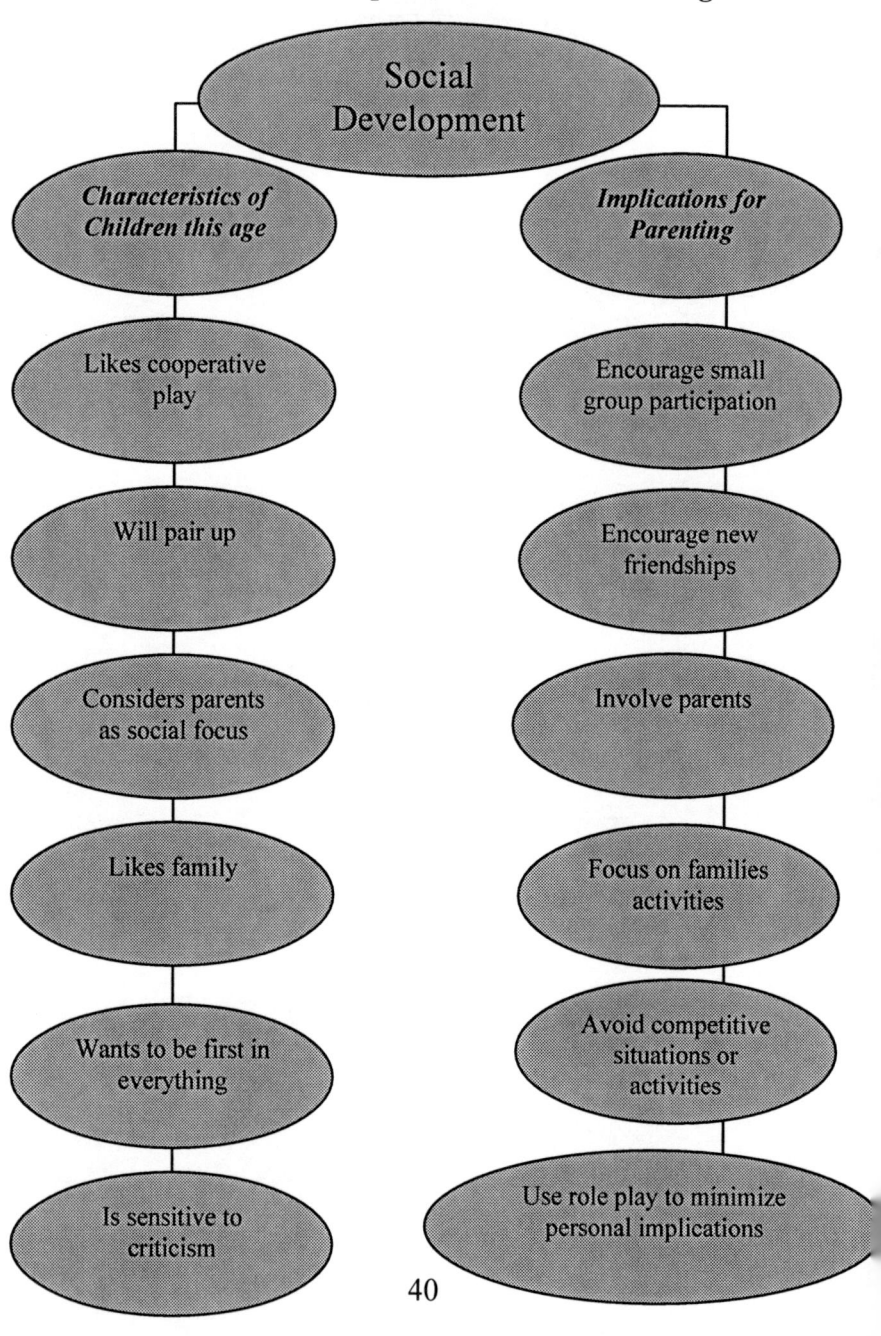

Illustration 4
Characteristics and Implications for Children Ages 5-6

Social Development

Characteristics of Children this age

- Likes cooperative play
- Will pair up
- Considers parents as social focus
- Likes family
- Wants to be first in everything
- Is sensitive to criticism

Implications for Parenting

- Encourage small group participation
- Encourage new friendships
- Involve parents
- Focus on families activities
- Avoid competitive situations or activities
- Use role play to minimize personal implications

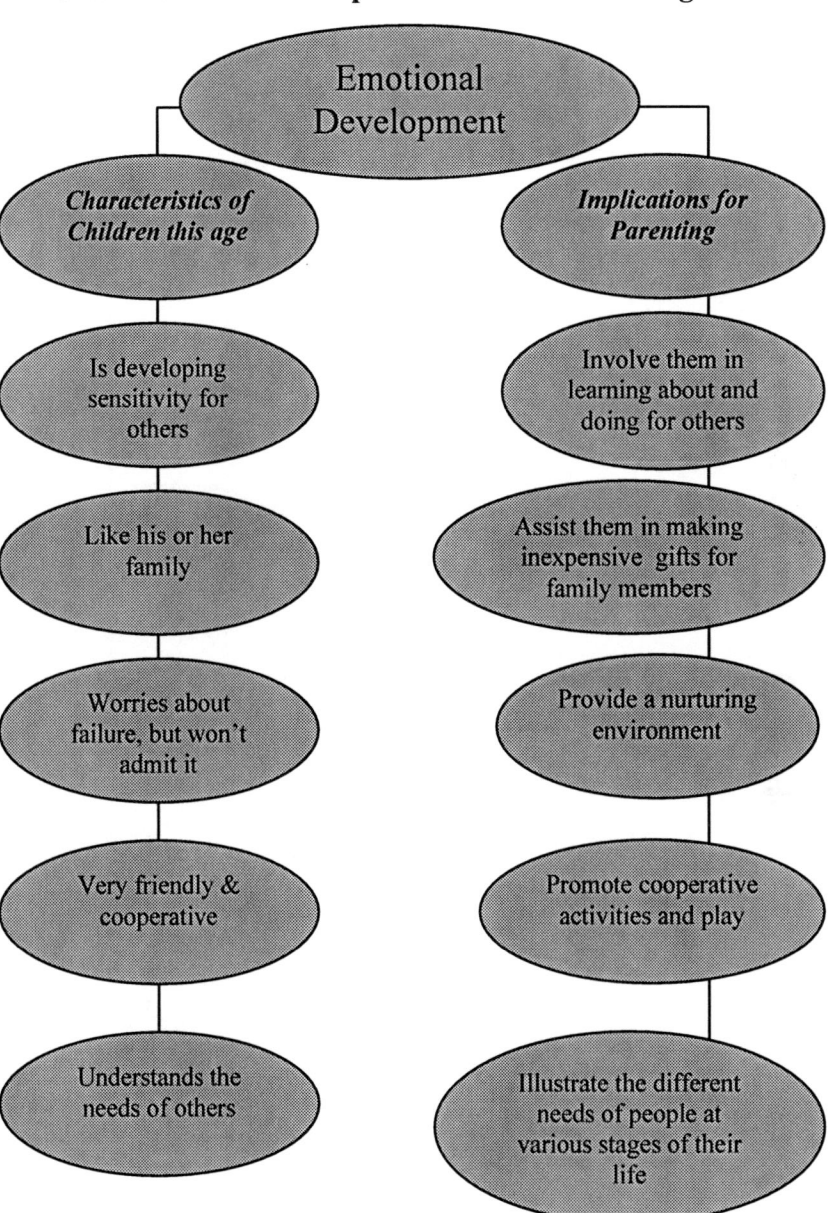

Illustration 5
Characteristics and Implications for Children Ages 7-8

Emotional Development

Characteristics of Children this age

- Is developing sensitivity for others
- Like his or her family
- Worries about failure, but won't admit it
- Very friendly & cooperative
- Understands the needs of others

Implications for Parenting

- Involve them in learning about and doing for others
- Assist them in making inexpensive gifts for family members
- Provide a nurturing environment
- Promote cooperative activities and play
- Illustrate the different needs of people at various stages of their life

CREATIVELY EXPLORING

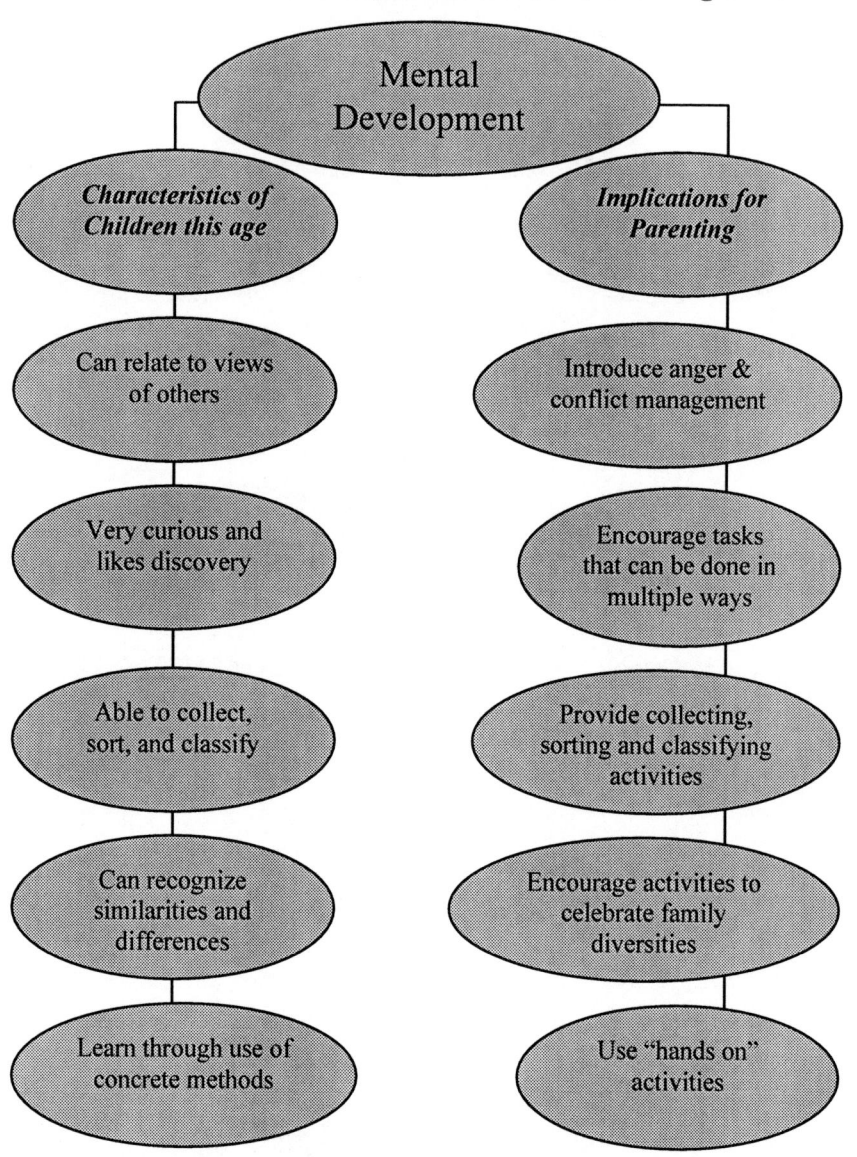

Illustration 6
Characteristics and Implications for Children Ages 7-8

Mental Development

Characteristics of Children this age

- Can relate to views of others
- Very curious and likes discovery
- Able to collect, sort, and classify
- Can recognize similarities and differences
- Learn through use of concrete methods

Implications for Parenting

- Introduce anger & conflict management
- Encourage tasks that can be done in multiple ways
- Provide collecting, sorting and classifying activities
- Encourage activities to celebrate family diversities
- Use "hands on" activities

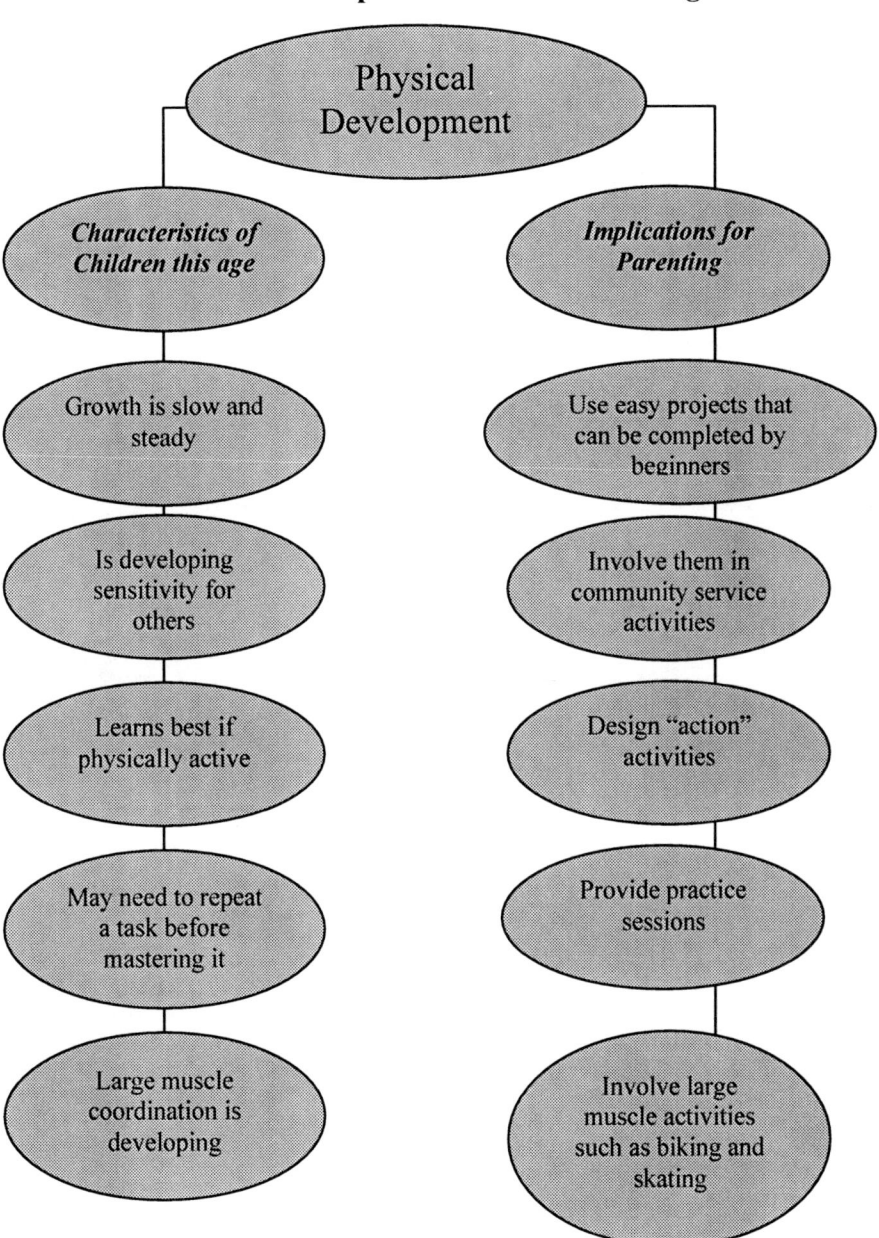

Illustration 7
Characteristics and Implications for Children Ages 7-8

Physical Development

Characteristics of Children this age

- Growth is slow and steady
- Is developing sensitivity for others
- Learns best if physically active
- May need to repeat a task before mastering it
- Large muscle coordination is developing

Implications for Parenting

- Use easy projects that can be completed by beginners
- Involve them in community service activities
- Design "action" activities
- Provide practice sessions
- Involve large muscle activities such as biking and skating

CREATIVELY EXPLORING

Illustration 8
Characteristics and Implications for Children Ages 7-8

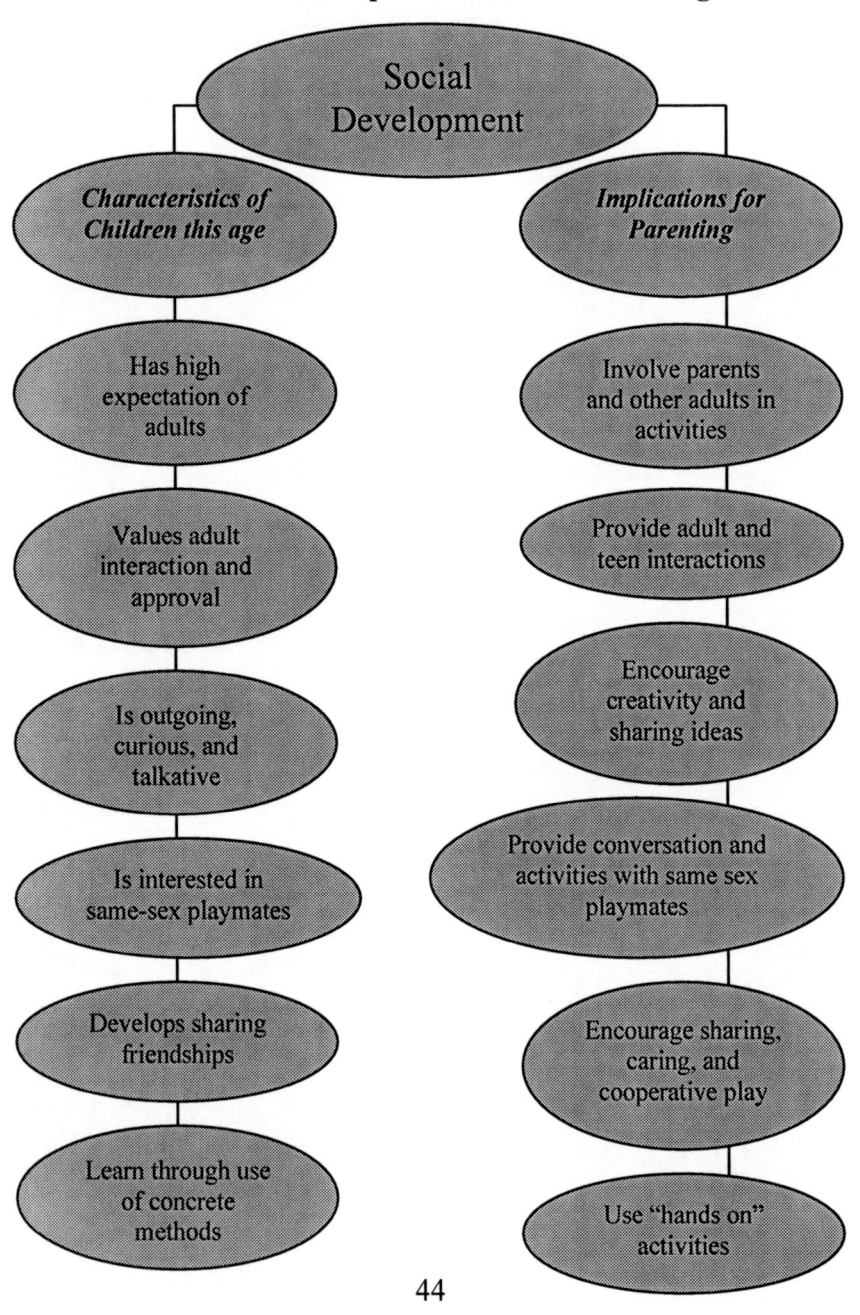

Social Development

Characteristics of Children this age

- Has high expectation of adults
- Values adult interaction and approval
- Is outgoing, curious, and talkative
- Is interested in same-sex playmates
- Develops sharing friendships
- Learn through use of concrete methods

Implications for Parenting

- Involve parents and other adults in activities
- Provide adult and teen interactions
- Encourage creativity and sharing ideas
- Provide conversation and activities with same sex playmates
- Encourage sharing, caring, and cooperative play
- Use "hands on" activities

CHAPTER 3

Creating a Learning Environment at Home

It is important for parents to be mindful of the growth and development of children as activities are implemented. A learning environment at home should accommodate children's eagerness for new experiences, their need for physical activity, their desire for the affection and attention from adults, and their inability to accept failure. Helping children ages 5-to-8 learn is an exciting, active, and stimulating experience. Parents and other adults are tremendously influential in helping children feel good about who they are and what they can do. **Learning activities will be positive experiences for children if the following are included:**

- Create a comfortable learning environment. Children tend to be comfortable and more creative in learning environments where adults are warm and encouraging, with many concrete materials and activities which are challenging, rewarding, expressive, and open-ended; and in which sufficient time and freedom exist for children to learn and practice skills at their own pace.

CREATIVELY EXPLORING

- Involve children in selecting and planning activities. Involvement in the selection of learning activities builds confidence, fosters personal initiative, and encourages the development of curiosity and creativity.

- To meet the needs and interests of children, make changes in activities often. Offering a broad variety of learning activities and experiences will sustain interest and involvement.

- Encourage children to talk and express their ideas. Children talk as they learn and learn best when they are involved in activities that allow them to practice, demonstrate, explain, and apply their learning.

- Limit activities to short time periods. Children ages 5- to-8 should not be expected to engage in one type of activity for too long. Incorporate quiet activities with those that require movement and active participation.

- Foster self-understanding by nurturing creativity and curiosity, and helping children see and appreciate the differences and similarities among people.

- Utilize every possible opportunity to help children develop communication skills, including listening skills, working together cooperatively, sharing, and conflict resolution emanating from words rather than physical confrontation.

- Provide opportunities, in secure situations and settings with guidance, for practicing sound problem-solving and decision-making.

- Provide an atmosphere that enhances children's ability to ask questions, identify and locate resources, think critically, and utilize their senses.

- Provide opportunities for children to develop control of their small muscles — using pencils, scissors, small utensils, and other tools. Games and recreation involving running, skipping, or hopping also encourage muscle development.

- Choose activities that promote and encourage cooperation rather than competition, involve developmentally appropriate skills, provide an opportunity for social interaction, and help children learn about fairness.

- Make sure learning experiences for children are developmentally and age appropriate while providing many opportunities to explore, inquire, and discover. Effective activities accommodate different kinds and levels of play, and promote physical, social, emotional, as well as cognitive development.

- Compliment your child every day by saying something positive to bolster their self-confidence. Make sure that structured recreation is a part of your children's learning experience. It is important to the growth and development of children ages 5-to-8 years of age. The recreational/play period *may* include games, puzzles, activities, or other types of active experiential involvement. The time allowed for play may be different at various times, but should last at least 15—20 minutes.

CREATIVELY EXPLORING

- Design activities and experiences that promote and build self-esteem by including opportunities to make choices and decisions, provide a sense of belonging, contribution, trust, promote responsibility, self-discipline, and self-control.

Recommended Educational Activities for Children Ages 5-to-8

5-Year-Olds
- Modeling clay
- Science materials (e.g. magnets, flashlights, docks and cars with see-through mechanisms Doll houses with furniture and people

6-Year-Olds
- Jigsaw puzzles
- Skipping ropes (jump ropes)
- Crafts involving small-muscle coordination (e.g. loop looms, spool knitting, stringing beads)
- Miniature forts, filling stations, farms

7-Year-Olds
- Board games, dominoes
- Doctor and nurse accessories
- Paper dolls
- Erector sets

8-Year-Olds
- Costumes and accessories of all sorts
- Board games which depend on skill as well as luck (e.g. checkers)

Recreational Puzzles and Games

Puzzles provide excellent opportunities for the development of intellectual skills, which are important in later life Puzzles give

practice with one form of sensory-motor coordination — eye-hand coordination. The child spots the correct puzzle piece then processes this visual information in his brain, makes the motor response of picking it up and places it in its proper position. Puzzles also help children:
- See spatial relationships — "seeing" abstractly in the mind that a particular piece fits in a certain spot.
- Develop attention span — the ability to work for a long time at a particular activity.
- Exercise small muscles located in the fingers.
- Improve visual scanning — involving the small muscles of the eyes. (This is an important skill in reading, as the eyes must move back and forth across the lines continuously)
- Develop problem-solving skills. Each time the child fits in a piece, he is solving a "mini-problem" that will contribute to the solution of the overall puzzle. Children get a tremendous feeling of accomplishment at finishing a puzzle, whether it is completing a four-piece puzzle or one with 500 pieces.

Suitable puzzles for the 5 and 6 year-old include brightly colored puzzles consisting of 15 to 50 pieces. The 7 and 8 year-old will feel comfortable with puzzles consisting of 50 to 100 pieces.

Games offer children entertainment and diversion. They also provide mental stimulation, social interaction, and a setting conducive to cooperative behavior. Games for children ages 5-to-8 should not have requirements which exceed their capabilities. This will cause frustration and misuse of the games rather than presenting the child with a challenge. If a parent plays with the child, some of the complicated skills can be circumvented. Games for this age group should help the player develop skills, such as problem-solving, decision-

CREATIVELY EXPLORING

making, or "putting himself/herself in his/her opponent's place" in order to develop a competing or blocking strategy. They should be intellectually stimulating and enjoyable. It is a good idea to note the manufacturers suggested age recommendations.

Race Games: With this type of game, there is generally a finish line of some kind, and the player moves along a path or through a maze to get to it. These games are good for young children because they focus only on one thing at a time - getting to the finish line.

Positional or Configurational Games: The player tries to get his or her pieces into a specified design. These games help children learn to identify different shapes and designs.

Accumulation Games: These call for the collection of game pieces of some kind. They help teach basic counting skills and recognition of masses. Children ages 5-to-8 enjoy collecting and sorting.

Games That Require Eye-Hand Coordination or Balance Skills: These include any game that calls for various types of eye-hand coordination.

Electronic Games: Many electronic games promote a number of important developmental skills. They give practice in eye-hand coordination and help to develop intellectual skills such as memorization, spelling, decision-making, mathematics and strategic thinking.

The overwhelming array of today's electronic games can be grouped into five broad categories:
- spoils
- target
- horoscope
- deduction/memory/strategy
- educational

The deduction/memory/strategy and educational games are the best buys for young children. These games develop skills, while still being interesting and challenging.

Using the Experiential Learning Model to Teach Critical Thinking

Learning theories provide a theoretical framework for helping children and adults learn. By understanding and applying learning theories, it is possible to help children learn more quickly, and help them better retain knowledge. There are five general learning strategies that parents should keep in mind at all times when dealing with children ages 5-to-8:

- Set clear and simple educational goals.
- Build a relationship between new and old knowledge.
- Organize experiential learning consisting of related parts.
- Be aware of the developmental needs of the child.
- Relate new information and skills to the real world.

The experiential learning model provides a framework for use with children involved in cooperative, experiential (hands-on) activities. This chapter explores the five steps in the experiential learning model for children ages 5-to-8. The experiential learning model has been widely recognized as one of the best approaches to helping children "learn by doing." Experiential learning occurs when children are involved in an activity, share the results with others, look back at it critically, determine what was useful, connect the experience to real-life situations, and use this information to perform another activity. Many outstanding children development programs in North Carolina and other states advocate experiential learning as the primary format for educating children. This model is used throughout the activities in this chapter to facilitate learning

CREATIVELY EXPLORING

and skill development for children ages 5 to 8.

Five key steps are a part of the experiential model. These steps include having the children:
- **Experience** the activity by performing or doing it.
- **Share** the results, reactions, and observations with others.
- **Process** the information through discussion, reflection, and analysis.
- **Generalize** the information to connect experiences to real-life situations.
- **Apply** what was learned to another situation that was experienced earlier.

Some steps in experiential learning may not present problems for most children, while some steps may require more assistance from parents. Developmentally, children ages 5 and 6 will be able to experience an activity and share it with others. Children ages 7 and 8 will be able to go further and may be able to analyze, generalize, or process the activity. Parents should be aware that they will need to provide assistance when children are being introduced and acclimated to experiential learning.

If an activity is kept at the appropriate level of experience, a child is able to process the information resulting from it. For example, a 7-year-old who helps his mother measure ingredients for a recipe at home can internalize that experience and translate it into another measuring experience at school. The child may tell his parent when they are making a fruit salad that, "I learned how to use a measuring cup when assisting grandmother put bubble bath gels in my bathtub." This example demonstrates that the child was able to generalize and apply the measuring experience to another experience.

DR. SHIRLEY B. MCNEILL

Recognizing and Encouraging Young Children

The effective use of recognition and awards motivate children and adults. Recognition motivates children to excel, and encourages them. Additionally, it supports the efforts of children and adults as they engage in individualized and group learning. It also increases their interest and may serve to help them learn.

Recognizing an individual for an accomplishment and showing appreciation to people who helped in some way are important jobs for parents as well as for the children themselves. Appropriate recognition for children varies according to stage of development, age, past experiences, personal interests, family lifestyles, community, and cultural heritage. It is necessary to constantly update recognition and award incentives to ensure that the recognition awarded is important to the children. Because children are growing emotionally, socially, mentally, and physically and are developing skills at different times, using standards for participation is a positive recognition strategy. Standards and effective communication can be used to help children learn new skills and behaviors as they grow and develop.

Standards for Recognition for Young Children
1. Involve children in the process.
2. Help them agree upon goals.
3. Remind the family members that the ultimate goal is not recognition, but to learn to work together.
4. Recognize all members and children involved.
5. Set simple criteria for earning recognition.
6. Give recognition as it is earned.

Recognition for Children Ages 5-to-8
Parents who are interested in fostering character development at a young age should promote and encourage cooperative

CREATIVELY EXPLORING

group learning; therefore, group and individual recognitions for achievement are encouraged. In recognizing children on an individual basis, remember that children at this age are developing skills and abilities at different levels and times. When children work together, they examine their own skills and abilities, and explore solutions beyond their own ideas. Recognition for achievements doesn't have to be a grand event. However, it should occur often during each learning experience. The most successful form of recognition for children ages 5-to-8 is recognition that is immediate in nature. Parents should try to give each child a positive response and provide reinforcement for the activities and social skills accomplished. Because children at this age have a high sense of right and wrong, and of justice and injustice, it is tremendously important that they understand the guidelines for participation. They must understand why recognition is given; the standards used, and believe that the recognition is warranted. For example, when Jacques receives a sticker because she showed a lamb, and her brother was unable to show one, it is important to help both Jacques and her brother know why only one child received a sticker.

Using a variety of strategies and techniques to recognize children for their accomplishments is very memorable and effective for showing appreciation for the 5-to-8 year old. Since we spend a great deal of time conversing, using communications to recognize children is a practical concept. We use communications to transfer knowledge, to comfort, to stimulate or influence, to express an emotion, or to convey authority. Now we will use it to send clear messages to more effectively recognize children. Since we communicate in many ways, a focus on communicating for recognition will help us convey encouragement and enhance listening.

The success of cooperative learning depends on how well children have been prepared to work together. Discouraged children, who have experienced failure in school or in groups, need the reassurance that cooperative learning offers them. It also offers an encouraging environment that promotes success. Successful children know that cooperative learning does not threaten their success. Cooperative activities and learning are significant components for children growth and development. Children ages 5-to-8 are beginning to define their standards and value the presence and opinions of adults; therefore, it is important to make sure that all children are recognized fairly. Recognizing children using positive communications and standards are appropriate ways to respond to children in learning settings. These recognition methods may take more time initially; however, children will increase their quality and quantity of interactions.

Standards

Using standards to recognize children will provide a perimeter to use as children plan and work toward their goals, skills, and desired behaviors. A standard is the criteria used to evaluate a product, a skill, or a behavior. Usually there is more than one quality to be considered in establishing standards.

Standards help children evaluate the skills they are learning. Standards are derived from research and are useful as children begin their work on a task, project, or goal. Standards provide a systematic approach to discuss with children how well they have achieved their goals and ways to make improvements. Using standards helps children increase their skills in establishing their own standards. They position themselves to assist other children and adults in establishing standards. Standards can also be used to measure progress, define expectations, describe quality, and provide consistent feedback. Using standards provides a constructive and organized opportunity for discussions and interaction between parents and children. Once standards are set,

CREATIVELY EXPLORING

enforced, understood, and accepted, using them in encouraging children becomes easier.

Encouragement

Encouragement is the recommended method for recognizing participation, achievement, work well done, peer competition, peer conflict, and progress toward goals. Using encouragement lets children know that what they do is separate from who they are. It conveys that they, as a person, are good enough as they are. It encourages children to identify their own strengths and build on them. Encouragement also shows faith in children that enables them to have faith in themselves and utilizes the interests of the child to energize experiential learning.

Encouragement can be used for participation and cooperation recognition by using a three-step communication method including:
- **Describe** in simple and clear terms the action you seek to recognize by explaining what you see and how it made you feel.
- **Encourage self-praise** for children by asking them what do you think of your action?
- **End with a short summary** using one to three words, such as Great Job!

If parents decide to use ribbons as a form of recognition, consider using ribbons of the same color and discourage competitiveness among the children. Children will quickly notice different colors and the meaning or significance of varying colors.

Individual Recognition

Individual recognition should be given to children for their participation, cooperation, achievements, and work well done. Make sure the children understand the standards for their recognition and why they are being recognized.

Some of the forms of recognition may include:
- Sharing a special project with other children
- Leading an activity or game
- Complimenting children in the presence of their peers or at an unexpected time, such as during refreshment or recreation period
- Certificates
- Caps and t-shirts
- Stickers
- Useful memorabilia
- Buttons
- Vests
- Collectibles

Group Recognition

Group recognition can be given to two or more children for birthday celebrations, family reunions and other gatherings for their participation in cooperative group activities. It is important to help children become interested in cooperating and sharing group successes. This cooperation is likely to encourage children to assist each other, because they will come to realize that helping and working with others can benefit both them and the members of their group. Make sure that children understand why their group is getting collective recognition, so cooperative behavior will receive positive reinforcement. These awards may be given less frequently than the individual awards, because group dynamics and processes take longer. Quarterly or four main awards to the group per year are appropriate.

CREATIVELY EXPLORING

Recognition might include:

- Trip to their favorite fast-food place, skating rink, or amusement park
- Surprising them with a "You Are Special" pizza party
- Assembling the children in a circle, telling what contribution they made to the group and why their contribution is important and asking others to applaud
- Allow the group to lead a song or activity
- Group certificates
- Group newspaper articles
- Caps with their name on it
- T-shirts with their name on it
- Useful group memorabilia
- Group ribbons
- Stickers or buttons
- Collectibles

Enhancing Character Development While Showing Children Love

Take advantage of every opportunity to identify and acknowledge your child's **"Uniqueness"**. Create special birthday celebrations, family traditions on holidays, and schedule special time with each child and let the focus be on them.

Share your values with your children. Whether values are shared or not, children will know what is important to family members by actions, rituals, and responses to certain events and people. Discussing values will provide children with a clearer vision of the significance of your personal beliefs.

Young children really value and want **consistency**. Make it a point to be consistent in your daily routines, time of meals, quality time together, discipline and other family functions because children need to be able to count on some things being the same.

Make a habit of **being kind, honest, and trustworthy** to others on a daily basis. As children gather information to understand the world and feel comfortable in their environment, they are modeling your every action and behavior. They will learn what is taught to them by your actions, attitudes, and behaviors.

Praise children with words such as: I appreciate your persistence, I'm proud of you, you're precious, you're my treasure, you mean a lot to me, you are fun, you're a joy.

Encourage children with words such as: You're catching on, I trust you, you're really thinking now, and other descriptive words to give your approval such as: terrific, fantastic, cool, amazing, and incredible!

Help children build **healthy self-esteem** by providing them with: a sense of security, a feelings of belonging, a sense of trust, opportunities to make choices, an environment that promotes acceptance, and a safe place to explore while taking risks.

Be **responsible to society**, if you know or think your child has a social, cognitive, or mental problem; please get help as soon as possible. Parents intuitively know the characteristics of normal behavior. I have never heard the parents of a murderer express surprised by their son's or daughter's actions.

Express your true feelings to your children. It teaches them honesty and lets them know that mistakes are acceptable. Young children understand, I'm sorry, thank you, I love you, I am proud of you, and I misunderstood your intentions.

CHAPTER 4

Experientially Enhancing Character

At one time helping children develop cognitively was all that was necessary to ensure their success as well rounded children, well behaved teens and competent, caring, and responsible adults. As social, family, and environmental needs change, preparing children for the future includes the development of emotional and social as well as cognitive skills. Studies are finding that character development is as critical to a successful future as cognitive development. Character development begins at home with parents taking the lead. At home character development activities and reinforcements can have a positive and long-lasting influence on the 5-to-8 year old. Teaching and reinforcing social skills at early ages may decrease or eliminate many negative at risk behaviors and some "acting out" that appears in older children. Many attitudes, habits, and behaviors are acquired by children very early in their life span.

PARENTS PLEASE TEACH YOUR CHILD HOW TO LOVE, VALUE, NURTURE, AND RESPECT

CREATIVELY EXPLORING

THEMSELVES AT AN EARLY AGE. PARENTS SHOULD MODEL LOVING, VALUING, NURTURING AND RESPECTING SELF DAILY SO THAT YOUNG CHILDREN WILL LEARN AND MODEL THESE ACTIONS. IN ADDITION TO MODELING, MAKE A SPECIAL EFFORT TO ENSURE THAT THESE ACTIONS ARE REWARDED AND REINFORCED.

Research shows that children who lie most are more likely to come from homes in which parents frequently tell lies. In addition, children who come from homes with minimal supervision or where there is parental rejection are more frequently dishonest. Although few parents would say they ever lie, you should be aware of the direct or indirect effects that lying has on children. There is never a good reason to lie to your children. This does not mean you should tell them everything - there are many things they don't need to know, however, there is no need to ever tell them a fabrication. If something is private or beyond your children's understanding, tell them just that.

When you're teaching honesty, caring/kindness, or manners make these a priority in your home, reinforce positive behaviors with praise and approval and discourage negative behaviors with immediate reprimands and consequences. When you feel rules and teachings have been learned, add another three to five to the list. With some children, you may need to continue the list in this manner, but for the most part, they want to please adults. If you make your expectations clear, then consistently reinforce and model new behaviors, you will find that children will seek opportunities to let you know that they have learned the things you are teaching.

This chapter is designed to help children develop competencies in social interaction, decision-making, responsibility, respect for self and others, trustworthiness, fairness, diversity and citizenship. The activities in this book are designed with special emphasis on experiential learning using a variety of learning activities. The activities are designed to help children develop one or more "life skills" related to Character Development. "Life skills" are abilities, knowledge, attitudes or behaviors that enable children to manage real-life situations and transitions. Many of the activities are self-contained: you will need nothing more than this guidebook and common household items to lead your child through them.

Each activity contains eight sections. The first three sections are the objectives, materials needed, and background information. The background section is written as a lead-in to introduce the subject, giving information that can be read to the children to start a discussion before the activity is experienced. It is designed to provide parents with researched background so that they do not need to go to the library for information before starting the experience. The fourth section has detailed instructions for the activity, and it is at this point that the "experiential learning process" begins. In the experiential learning process, the activity is an experience for children. Experiential learning does not stop with the experience alone, the final four sections-sharing, processing, generalizing, and applying are equally important. These final four sections provide eight questions which the child should be asked, to help them critically think through their experience and evaluate it.

Each activity has two questions related to sharing, processing the information to help children discuss the results of the experience and reflect why the results happened. The next level of critical thinking is generalizing the information to help children connect the experience to another real-life experience. Finally, through applications, children are able to transfer what was learned to another situation that is similar. After going through the eight sharing, processing, generalizing, and applying questions, add at least two additional questions of your own to each of the listed questions to personalize the

CREATIVELY EXPLORING

learning experience to your child's family, and community environment. This can easily be done by changing out one of the words in the question. It is not necessary to ask your child all these questions the first time you discuss the topic, maybe ask two questions a day or setting. Spreading the questions out over a period of a week or so will allow your child time to think and reflect on the topic.

This experiential unit is divided into two sections, the first section deals with understanding, valuing, and respecting self. Activities are focused on definitions and learning about honesty, being responsible, respecting self, expressing uniqueness through clothing, family celebrations, handling emotions, and dealing with anger. The first section is designed for 7 & 8 year olds. The second section, designed for 5 & 6 year olds, deals with understanding, valuing, and respecting others. Specifically, children are exposed to understanding likenesses and differences, respecting others, ethnicity, the Golden Rule, complimenting others, caring for friends, coping with bullies, and goal-setting. There is one paper and pencil activity that relates to and to support each of the activities in both the sections. At the end of both sections, a list of parent/child activities is given to provide additional experiences to enhance character development. A Glossary of Character terms follows the child/parent activities to assist in defining terms used in this chapter.

Activity 1: Building Blocks to Honesty

Objective: Your child will learn key elements to building trust by determining ways to earn it.

Materials Needed:
- Small cubed building blocks (one for each child)

- Index cards cut down to the size of the building blocks
- Tape
- Crayons

Background:
Being honest is a first step toward developing trust. When you trust someone you know you can count on them to be honest and not let you down. When a person is honest, they tell the truth. They do not cheat, or steal. Sometimes it may be difficult to make a clear distinction between make believe and reality, lying and telling the truth, and understanding that dishonesty can be hurtful to others. Telling a lie is saying something that you know is not true. Lies are told for different reasons, including to make yourself look better, to avoid punishment or other consequences of your actions, or to keep from sharing. Cheating or doing something not fair while playing games is being dishonest. Breaking the rules or changing the rules after a game starts is unfair and another form of cheating. The most courageous and safest practice is to be honest, which at times is not always the easier course of action to take. If you cheat, lie, or steal it doesn't mean that you are a bad person, it means that you have made bad decisions which will make it difficult for others to trust your judgment and decisions.

Experience:
1. Give each child an index card and crayons and have them draw pictures of following instructions given by their parents such as; picking up their toys; practicing honesty or kind deeds. Have them share their pictures with the others.
2. Use the cards to make a large tower. Tape each card to a building block and carefully stack them to form a pyramid shaped tower.
3. After tower is built, remind children that trust is like this tower, it takes a long time to build trust but it

doesn't take long to destroy trust. Illustrate how it weakens trust by pulling another block from the tower. (when you are not honest, lie, cheat, steal, or be unfair) Continue with examples until your tower crumbles.

Share:
1. What happens to trust when you are not honest?
2. What happens to trust when you are unfair?

Process:
1. What actions have you taken to establish trust from your parents?
2. How have you established trust at school?

Generalize:
1. Can you remember another time when you slowly built trust that was destroyed quickly?
2. What will you do to show your parents you can be trusted?

Analyze:
1. How have you shown that you can be trusted at home?
2. What has a friend done recently to build your trust in them?

Writing about Honesty

Directions: Copy the sentence below on a sheet of paper; use dotted lines so that children can trace the letters. Ask them to trace the sentence describing honest actions and then ask children to discuss with you how they feel about the statements.

> *Honest boys and girls are always truthful. They tell the truth every day. Even when telling the truth may get them or their friends in trouble*

DR. SHIRLEY B. MCNEILL

Activity 2: Printing for Respect

Objective: Your children will appreciate and respect themselves.

Materials Needed:
- Art supplies
- Finger paint
- White paper

Background:
You are very special and a wonderfully unique person. There is not another person in the world that is exactly like you!!! Respecting yourself and being good to yourself plays an important role in how you treat others. Respecting others is illustrated through the use of good manners, positive actions and attitudes, showing consideration of others' feelings, and dealing responsibly with anger and disagreements. In order to respect others, you must first respect yourself. Taking care of your body by washing your hands often, brushing your teeth daily, and good grooming are ways to show respect for your body. In order to improve your self respect, consider taking a quick self-assessment. Think about new ways to show respect for self and others, think about what makes you feel special, what have you done to make someone else feel special, what makes you feel bad, and what have you done to make someone feel bad, and what are your special abilities and what are the special abilities of your best friend? If you answered I don't know to any of these items, start to identify the answers to each of these questions and discuss them. (If they can't answer these questions, assist them in identifying and naming their special abilities and skills).

Experience:
1. What do thumbprints and snowflakes have in common? They are Unique. No two thumbprints or snowflakes

are the same. Help your child press their thumbs in some finger paint, and then on paper. Have them to observe their thumbprints.
2. After the thumbprints are dry, ask your child to use markers and crayons to turn the thumbprints into animals. Two thumbprints side by side become a butterfly with the addition of a body, head, antennae, and spots. Other easily made thumbprint animals are fish, ladybugs, bumblebees, frogs, mice, and spiders.

Share:
1. What did you notice about the thumbprint?
2. How was your thumbprint different from mother or father?

Process:
1. What do thumbprints tell us about each other?
2. How are thumbprints like people?

Generalize:
1. What are some other characteristics that make us different ?
2. How are you different from your brother, sister, or cousin?

Analyze:
1. What did you learn from this experience that could help you in school?
2. Why is it important to recognize the uniqueness of others?

Tracing Respectful Actions

Directions: Copy the words below on a sheet of paper; use dotted lines so that children can trace them. Ask them to trace the words describing respectful actions of family members or friends, then have them to write the name of a person in their family that the word on the list describes.

Considerate

Tolerant

Civility

Accepting

Mannerly

Activity 3: My Favorite Chores

Objective: Your child will learn the importance of being responsible, and how being irresponsible can affect others.

Materials Needed:
- Construction paper
- Small paper plates
- Scissors
- Crayons, pencils or markers
- Glue or tape

Background:
Years ago, almost all children had household chores that they had to complete after getting home from school. After school chores were and still are a good method to help children develop a strong sense of personal responsibility. Completing chores also helps in learning self-discipline, skill development, developing a healthy sense of self, and becoming more capable and independent. Another benefit of helping out around the house and at school is that it makes it easier to develop a sense of personal responsibility, while contributing to the family in meaningful

CREATIVELY EXPLORING

ways. Satisfactorily completing chores are a way to earn allowances or special privileges. When you or another family member drops his or her responsibility and do not complete their chores, it affects the quality of enjoyment for the whole family. Think for a minute, how it would feel to have no food, shelter, clothing, toys, and transportation provided for you.

Experience:
1. Provide your children with a piece of construction paper. Ask them to draw five or six large flower petals on the construction paper.
2. Pass out a small paper plate, ask children to write "I am responsible" in the middle of the plate. Have them write something for which they are responsible for on each petal. (some may include picking up toys, cleaning their room, doing homework, etc.). After your children have written a responsibility on each petal, have them cut it out and glue or tape each petal around the edges of the paper plate to make a flower.

Share:
1. Name and describe the actions or things done by a responsible person in your family.
2. What can you be responsible for at home after school?

Process:
1. Could you remember to do some basic chores around the house?
2. Can you think of other things you can do at home that are not on your flower?

Generalize:
1. What would happen if you did not follow through and complete your chores?
2. What would happen if your mother did not follow through and complete her chores?

Analyze:
1. Do you see any chores you can add to your list in the future?
2. What would happen if your father, mother or guardians stopped working?

CREATIVELY EXPLORING

Responsible Behavior Traits

Directions: Find and circle the responsible behavior traits in the hidden words list.

Hidden Words

fair	caring	respectful
reliable	discipline	persevere
diligent		

	1	2	3	4	5	6	7	8	9	10	11	12	13	14	15	16	17
1	U	N	B	R	A	I	N	W	S	O	H	I	Q	Y	Z	A	I
2	B	I	L	R	M	A	D	P	E	O	E	N	I	L	M	A	P
3	O	D	E	E	L	J	E	U	A	R	S	M	R	D	V	F	T
4	N	G	E	S	Q	Y	Z	A	I	U	W	S	O	H	I	B	N
5	J	E	U	P	O	P	D	C	X	T	U	K	A	R	S	O	P
6	C	X	C	E	T	U	I	K	L	M	R	D	V	F	T	N	G
7	U	D	A	C	F	U	L	N	B	R	A	I	N	W	S	O	H
8	I	I	R	T	Q	Y	I	Z	P	A	I	B	I	L	M	A	D
9	P	S	I	F	E	O	G	R	E	L	I	A	B	L	E	E	N
10	I	C	N	U	L	M	E	A	R	F	A	I	R	P	O	D	E
11	L	I	G	L	J	E	N	U	S	A	R	S	M	R	D	V	F
12	T	P	N	G	E	Q	T	Y	E	Z	A	I	U	W	S	O	H
13	I	L	B	N	J	E	U	O	V	P	C	X	T	U	K	A	R
14	S	I	O	P	C	X	T	U	E	K	L	M	R	D	V	F	T
15	N	N	G	U	F	U	N	B	R	R	A	I	N	W	S	O	H
16	I	E	Q	Y	Z	A	I	B	E	I	L	M	A	D	P	E	O
17	E	N	I	L	M	A	P	O	D	E	L	J	E	U	A	R	S
	1	2	3	4	5	6	7	8	9	10	11	12	13	14	15	16	17

Activity 4: Dressing With Uniqueness

Objective: Your child will design a shirt that showcases their uniqueness.

Materials Needed:
- Crayons or Markers
- Paper with shirt outline

Background:
Clothing needs change as we grow and develop. The clothes you are wearing are probably durable, colorful, versatile, and color coordinated. The type and style of clothing worn by adults is very different. Occupation, lifestyle, climate, and gender influence clothing. The clothing we wear has many functions. Clothing that you selected to wear today are worn to cover and protect your body. Clothes are also worn as self expressions, for safety, to identify different cultures, and for job recognition such as policemen and nurses. The military uses clothes as a protective measure to camouflage their presence. Clothes worn in this state may be different from those worn in other states, due to the climate. Your clothes consist of your favorite colors, styles, and accessories. Clothes can help us feel special, and some can even make us feel more confident!

Experience:
1. Ask your child to color the shirt outline based on the following guideline. Color the collar of the shirt according to their birthday month: January–dark blue; February-red; March-purple; April-color of your choice; May-gray; June-orange; July-yellow; August-pink; September-light green; October-black; November–light blue; and December-dark green.
2. On the right sleeve, children will draw one stripe to

CREATIVELY EXPLORING

represent each sister or female cousin. On the left sleeve, draw one stripe for each brother or male cousin.
3. On the bottom border of the shirt tell the child to draw their pets.
4. Add other ideas as you wish and then have them display their shirts.

Share:
1. Did you like the shirt you designed?
2. Will you wear the shirt for special occasions or everyday?

Process:
1. What did you learn about yourself by designing the shirt?
2. Why is it important to express your uniqueness?

Generalize:
1. What school event allowed you to express yourself through clothing?
2. Have you ever gone to a costume party?

Analyze:
1. If you had to design something else, what would it be?
2. How would you design a shirt to represent the state of North Carolina?

Spelling Character Words

Directions: Fill in the missing letter for the listed character words.

fair_ess
respec_

DR. SHIRLEY B. MCNEILL

trustworthines◯

car◯ng

e◯hics

i◯tegrity

hones◯y

jus◯ice

toler◯nce

Activity 5: Helping and Practicing Responsible Behaviors

Objective:
Your child will be able to list helpful and responsible behaviors.

Materials Needed:
- Pictures of helpful situations - person picking up toys, paper, assisting an older person crossing the street, helping a friend to their feet that has fallen from their bicycle, others of your choice.
- Job chart (can be made out of fabric, or it can be on laminated paper)

Background:
Being responsible includes doing your fair share while managing your behaviors, feelings, and attitudes while contributing to the betterment of society. A responsible person accepts the consequences of their actions,

CREATIVELY EXPLORING

behaviors, and decisions. The consequences of good actions, behaviors, and decisions are rewards, recognition, and extra privileges. Good actions include picking up clothes, keeping your room clean, putting toys in your toy box, taking care of your pets, doing your homework, putting your clothes in the hamper, and assisting in household chores when your family need you, and behaving well in public. Negative actions are actions that are not acceptable by your parents, school, and your community. The consequences of negative actions, behaviors, and decisions are punishment, reprimands, and loss of privileges. Each individual is in charge of managing their actions, behaviors, and decisions as you make contributions to your home, school, and community. Behaving responsibly means that one is doing their fair share, using self-control, practicing self-discipline, and accepting the consequences of their actions while contributing to society.

Experience:
1. Read the poem or story from one of your child's books or magazines. Discuss the story or what's happening in the pictures of the magazines and identify as many helpful behaviors as possible.
2. Show pictures that illustrate peers being helpful. Ask your child to tell how the people pictured are being helpful.
3. Make a list of ways to show helpfulness. Go over the list with your child after you are finished looking at the pictures. Using the list ask your child to list ways that they can help at home.

Share:
1. Why are the things on the list of ways to show helpfulness?
2. What would happen if the things listed were not done?

Process:
1. Why it is good to be helpful at home, school or in the community?
2. Which of the pictures demonstrate some helpful roles you are already doing at home, school or in the community?

Generalize:
1. Did you learn new ways to be helpful at home or at school?
2. Make a list of jobs you need to fulfill at home and in your community.

Analyze:
1. Name ways you will contribute to helping at school next week, next month.
2. Name some things you can do to be helpful to another community.

CREATIVELY EXPLORING

Scrambling to Trustworthiness

Directions: Unscramble each of the words that describe the traits of a person who is worthy of trust. Copy the letters in the cells to create the word.

TEHNOSY	☐☐☐☐☐☐☐
TUARPLEEB	☐☐☐☐☐☐☐☐☐
EELILARB	☐☐☐☐☐☐☐☐
DOIKVNETO	☐☐☐☐☐☐☐☐☐
RITTYINEG	☐☐☐☐☐☐☐☐☐

Activity 6
Family Celebrations and Traditions

Objective:
Your child will share one of their favorite family celebrations.

Materials Needed:
- Large white construction paper (flip chart)
- Crayons or markers

DR. SHIRLEY B. MCNEILL

Background: Family celebrations and traditions are different for different families and are celebrated in different ways. The size of celebrations may be large, medium or small, depending on the size of families. Family traditions can teach values. For example, some families make it a tradition of helping neighbors, teaching caring, supporting older adults, participating in community service projects or promoting volunteerism. In some families it is a tradition to get together and talk about their best experience of the day or the past week or have a weekly family meeting. This is an opportunity to learn about what is important to other family members. Getting together not only helps us learn about our family values, but deepen family bonds, commitments, and unity while providing support and encouragement. Family traditions can include large annual gatherings such as family reunions, birthday parties, and special holiday activities during Easter, July 4th, Christmas, and Thanksgiving, to name a few. Smaller gatherings such as family meetings to discuss vacations and other issues are also traditions for some families.

Experience:
1. Discuss with your child the type of family and special celebrations that are recognized in your family. Include birthdays, graduations, weddings, anniversaries and others of your choice.
2. Ask your child to identify special celebrations they enjoy celebrating with their family. List their answers on the sheet of paper.
3. Have your child to draw two pictures of his or her family celebrating a special day and label the pictures. Refer to the list you made for ideas. Then have the child to share their pictures with you and another family member.

Share:
1. What are some of the special events people in your community celebrate?
2. What are some of your family traditions?

CREATIVELY EXPLORING

Process:
1. Name two family celebrations that are fun to you.
2. What is the name of a celebration of a culture that is different from your culture?

Generalize:
1. Discuss other special celebrations you would like to have with your family?
2. Have you ever attended a celebration with a family of a different culture?

Analyze:
1. What would you like to include in your family celebration to make it more special?
2. What is your favorite part of family celebrations?

Things Good Citizens Do

Directions: Place the citizenship words in alphabetical order.

Word List
Volunteer	vote	cooperate
Helpful	obey rules	lawful
Pay	taxes	recycle

_____

_____

_____

_____

_____

_____

DR. SHIRLEY B. MCNEILL

_____

_____

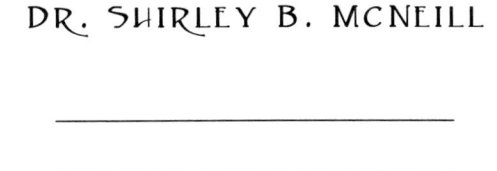

Activity 7: Responsibly Handling Emotions

Objective: Your child will practice techniques to handle negative emotions.

Materials Needed:
- Construction paper (12 sheets)
- Black marker

Background:
Emotions are feelings one may have that are either positive or negative, that can result from a variety of reasons such as stress, change in schedules, family transitions, poor school success, disagreement with siblings, happiness over a gift, joy over a new bicycle, or excitement about vacation plans. They are reactions to things or people in our life that cause discomfort, unhappiness, or happiness. By handling negative emotions responsibly, you will learn to refrain from screaming, having a temper tantrum, and crying when you don't get your way. Developing a healthy sense of managing emotions is as important as being at the school bus stop on time. Each child is responsible for managing their behaviors, attitudes, actions, and feelings. Accurately dealing with and expressing feelings gives emotional safety. No two people handle their emotions in exactly the same way. However, anger is expressed more among the 5- to 8 year old age group than any other emotion. Children are likely to hurt others' feelings with stinging words. Some of you will be guilty of teasing, insulting, nagging, and making fun of others. As you gain greater control of emotions by handling emotions responsibly, you are becoming more aware of how others feel.

CREATIVELY EXPLORING

Experience:
1. Give examples of good behaviors, or show a video if available. This activity will involve your child using their head to identify their emotions, heart to own their feelings, hands to actively control emotions, and improve their health by transforming negative feelings into positive actions.
2. On construction paper write the words- head, heart, hands and health, and situations of: "my friend broke a promise", "my parents were mean to me", "a classmate broke my favorite toy", "I missed the bus and had to walk to school", and my classmates hid my backpack. Add two of your choice.
3. Lead your child through role playing to handle emotions using their head, heart, hands, and health.

Share:
1. Describe how you used your head, heart, hands, and health to manage feelings of anger, disappointment, or bullying?
2. Why do you like using your head, heart, hands and health to manage feelings?

Process:
1. Why is it important to manage your emotions?
2. Describe how it made you feel when a friend did not manage their emotions?

Generalize:
1. How did you feel when a parent did not manage their emotions?
2. Have you seen someone on TV that did not manage their emotions? What happened?

Analyze:
1. What are additional things you can do to manage your

feelings of anger?
2. What are some things you can do to help someone else manage their emotions?

Writing Ways to NOT Handle your Emotions

Directions: Write the words below on a sheet of paper, on a board, or on a computer screen. Discuss with your child why these are not the ways to handle emotions, also discuss consequences of using these behaviors.

cry
tease
nag
tantrum
gossip
holler

Activity 8: Bag Up Anger

Objective: Your child will use role playing to practice strategies to deal with anger without using violence.

Materials Needed:
- Six unopened cans of different sizes
- Color construction paper
- Carrying sack or bag

Background:
Anger is a self-protective, emotional response to a hurt, pain, or threat. Its purpose is to protect one from harm. One may become angry because they feel or think they may be shortchanged, overlooked, or embarrassed. Anger is a natural emotion that is an unpleasant feeling and is often difficult to manage. Anger can generate very intense feelings in some

CREATIVELY EXPLORING

people, making them quick to "explode," "burn," or "boil over." We are responsible for controlling our angry feelings without breaking things or hurting other people by exhibiting violent behaviors. With effective anger management techniques, anger can be a socially accepted tool of self-protection. Instead of hitting, try cooling down by: writing on paper how you feel, counting to ten, repeating the names of your favorite family members, throw a ball and catch it five times, move away from the problem, or calmly tell the person you are angry and describe how you feel.

Experience:
1. Cover cans with paper and label each can with one of these incidents which can cause anger: not getting what I want, left out, ignored, called a bad name, someone stole my hat, falsely blamed, unfair punishment, making mistakes, and feeling jealous.
2. Ask your child to pick out the can or cans of feelings that he/she has felt that day or before, the month before, and the year before. Instruct your child to place the cans into the bag, (which gets heavier as cans are added).
3. Have the child to walk around the room experiencing the weight of the bag and how it grows heavier with the addition of each can.
4. Discuss the strategies to handle anger for each situation listed on the can. Strategies may include counting the things you are grateful for, reading a book, talking quietly about the problem, drawing an angry picture, molding clay, blowing up a balloon, writing a story about their anger, standing on one leg, or leaving situations that make you uneasy.

Share:
1. How did you feel when you thought about the incidents you placed in the bag?

2. Which type of anger provoking incident occurs most often with you?

Process:
1. Can you imagine carrying the weight of that bag each day?
2. Can you think of other incidents that have made you angry?

Generalize:
1. Describe additional ways to manage anger after this activity?
2. Who do you know that has managed their anger without violence?

Analyze:
1. What can you do in the future to manage angry feelings?
2. How can you help your siblings manage their angry feelings?

Handling Anger Feelings

Directions: Fill in the missing letter to write words that hinder dealing with anger.

Do Not:

insul◯

h◯t

thre◯ten

l◯e

b◯ame

CREATIVELY EXPLORING

dec**e**ive

st**e**al

Child/Parent Activities

1. Explore different topics and books about Character Development by visiting the public library.

2. Introduce your children to journaling to help them put their thoughts and feelings on paper.

3. Read to and with your children on a variety of topics including honesty, caring, respect, diversity, managing emotions, responsibility, and trust.

4. With the number of hours spent in front of the TV increasing for children, plan a no TV day. Play a variety of games, read books together, look at family photos, or exercise together.

5. Make a list of ten reasons why or how your child is special. Post the list on the refrigerator, in his/her room, or some very visible place. If you have more than one child, make a list for each of them and alternate posting them. Change the lists monthly.

6. Each day spend at least twenty minutes with each of your children doing fun things of their choice. After each activity, tell the children what they did well and celebrate their improvements!

7. Develop a list of family chores to help children develop skills and become a contributing member of their

family. Show children how to complete the chores and assign them chores appropriate for their age. Make sure you let them know how much you appreciate their input and reward them with privileges.

8. When you observe prejudice, bad manners, negative behaviors, and dishonesty, point out consequences of these actions with your children.

9. Model caring, positive communications, honesty, and kindness. Children are learning from us when we are teaching and when we are not teaching.

10. To increase your child's money management skills and understanding the value of money, consider starting an allowance by the time your child is seven. Give a weekly allowance the same day each week for the completion of specific chores/responsibilities.

Activity 1: We're Different, We're Alike

Objective: Assist your child describe the ways in which he/she is similar and different from others.

Materials Needed:
- Pencils
- Paper

Background: As humans, we are very much alike in some ways and are very different in other ways. All humans are basically alike because we have the ability to think, grow and change from year to year, share similar needs and drives, and are influenced by our environment as well as our heredity. Humans are different because of our personality, mental abilities, and physical appearance. Some

CREATIVELY EXPLORING

people are tall, short, have blonde hair, black hair, grey hair, multi-colored hair, others have long hair, short hair, some own pets, some reside in houses, apartments, others reside in townhouses, some families have two children, other families have four children, five children, and no children. There are many types of households: single, married, extended families; and many languages, including English, Spanish, and French. Being different is good because variance makes families, communities, schools, and the world very interesting. The unique qualities that every individual possess are special and should be valued, celebrated, and respected.

Experience:
1. Ask your child to think about ways in which they are similar to their classmates and ways in which they are different.
2. Get a sheet of paper to make a worksheet, title it: "All About Me". Write age, grade in school, hair color, number of brothers, number of sisters, name of my city, my favorite animal, my favorite food, my favorite book, and my favorite family member. Have your child to complete the worksheet and you complete one also.
3. Ask them to share the worksheet with a brother or sister and you.
4. Share and compare your differences and similarities from the worksheets.

Share:
1. What did you discover when you compared yourself to your parent?
2. What are the characteristics that you like about your parent?

Process:
1. What are some things about you that were the same as your brother/sister?
2. Did you find things about you that were different from your parent?

DR. SHIRLEY B. MCNEILL

Generalize:
1. What did you learn about yourself while completing the worksheet?
2. What did you learn about your parent while completing the worksheet?

Analyze:
1. How can you share with others that are different from you in the future?
2. Why is it important to understand and value people that are different from you?

Places to Learn about Others

Directions: Figure out the places code by placing a letter on the line to solve the riddle: These are places where we can go and visit to learn about the climate, language, literature, art, music, values, and habits of people that are different from you. (hint: there are 2 places)

__ __ __ __ __ __ ; __ __ __ __ __ __
8 37 28 3 37 8   34 5 29 1 17 1 12

17=A	2=K	30=H
29=B	34=L	19=V
10=C	8=M	3=W
16=D	24=N	32=X
3=E	4=O	12-Y
27=F	6=P	36=Z
31=G	14=Q	1=R
28=S	37=U	39=T
5=I		

CREATIVELY EXPLORING

Activity 2: Respecting Diversity

Objective: Your child will understand and respect differences between people.

Materials Needed:
- One potato per person (bag of white potatoes)
- A large bag

Background:
Understanding and respecting differences helps one learn more about people living in your community, school or church. When people are understood and tolerated it is easier to get along with them. When you see a person of a different ethnic group at school, say hello to them. Then start a conversation with them to understand more about them while telling them about your family, your family foods, family celebrations, family vacations, favorite music, and other special things about you and your family. The more you learn about people that are different from you the more comfortable you will become in their presence. Knowing the differences of other families, makes one more appreciative of our own family. Diversity is variety and differences that exist within languages, cultures, families, and individuals which brings a wealth of strengths and knowledge to society. There are many types of differences in height, gender, experiences, goals, size, hair color, skin color, religion, beliefs, values, and family lifestyles. Differences are not good or bad. Though people are different, everyone was born with the same value of worth and deserves an equal amount of respect. Differences are what makes life interesting and exciting and should be celebrated!

Experience:
1. Roll the potatoes out of the bag and ask your child to take one. Ask them to examine their potato, get to know

its bumps, scars, defects and make friends with it for one minute in silence so that they will be able to introduce their "potato friend".
2. After the silent period, ask your child to show the potato to you, introducing it with a little story of your choice on characteristics of your potato, then put the potato in the bag. Repeat this exercise until you notice your child is getting tired. After the potatoes are back in the bag, ask if they would agree with the statement, "all potatoes are the same." Why or Why not?
3. Ask your child if he/she think they could find their "potato friend" again. Take the potatoes out of the bag and invite the participants to pick out their "potato friend." There might be some difficulty and some last minute exchanging.
4. Tell the child: Perhaps potatoes are a little like people. We can lump people of a group all together. When we think, "they're all alike", we are really saying we haven't taken the time to get to know the person. When we do, we find out everyone is different and special in some way.

Share:
1. How did it feel to examine the potato for uniqueness and introduce it?
2. Was it difficult to find your "potato friend" among all the other the potatoes?

Process:
1. What problems can arise when you don't view each person as an individual?
2. Can you think of a time when you did not take time to get to know someone?

Generalize:
1. What did you learn about yourself through this activity?
2. How are people like potatoes?

CREATIVELY EXPLORING

Analyze:
1. How will you act differently in the future as a result of this activity?
2. Can you find pictures in a magazine or book that show different people?

Things that Create Diversity

Directions: From the Hidden Words list, circle the words of things that create diversity.

HIDDEN WORDS

| gender | height | beliefs |
| religion | families | goals |

	1	2	3	4	5	6	7	8	9	10	11	12	13	14	15	16	17
1	Y	Z	A	I	B	I	L	R	M	A	S	I	Z	E	D	P	E
2	O	E	N	I	L	M	A	E	P	O	D	E	G	L	J	E	U
3	A	R	S	F	A	M	I	L	I	E	S	M	O	R	D	V	F
4	T	N	G	E	Q	Y	Z	I	A	I	U	W	A	S	O	H	I
5	B	N	J	E	U	O	P	G	C	X	T	U	L	K	A	R	S
6	O	P	C	X	T	U	K	I	L	M	B	R	S	D	V	F	T
7	N	G	U	F	U	N	G	O	B	R	E	A	H	A	I	R	I
8	N	W	S	O	H	I	E	N	Q	Y	L	Z	A	I	B	I	L
9	M	A	D	P	E	O	N	H	S	K	I	N	E	N	I	L	M
10	A	P	O	D	E	L	D	E	J	E	E	U	A	R	S	M	R
11	D	V	F	T	N	G	E	I	E	Q	F	Y	Z	A	I	U	W
12	S	O	H	I	B	N	R	G	J	E	S	U	O	P	C	X	T
13	U	K	A	R	S	O	P	H	C	X	T	U	K	L	M	R	D
14	V	F	T	N	G	U	F	T	U	N	B	R	A	I	N	W	S
15	O	H	I	Q	Y	Z	A	I	B	I	L	M	A	D	P	E	O
16	E	N	I	L	M	A	P	O	D	E	L	J	E	U	A	R	S
17	M	R	D	V	F	T	N	G	E	Q	Y	Z	A	I	U	W	S

Activity 3: Exploring Other Cultures

Objective: Identify family cultures and differences between cultures of others.

Materials Needed:
- Sheet of paper
- Crayons or markers
- Flip chart
- Tape

Background:
Culture is a patterned way of behavior, language, and dress that is practiced within groups of people. Today, there are many cultures residing in North Carolina and other states. Individuals within each culture react, adjust, and develop adaptive reactions and coping strategies in their own particular, but special way. Every culture has values, beliefs, and norms embedded in language, religion, customs, and a variety of social organizations that are important to its members' behavior. Some of the cultures residing in North Carolina are African Americans, Asian Americans, European Americans, Hispanic Americans, and Native Americans. Our world is rapidly changing and our world's survival may depend on all cultures living and working harmoniously. Expand your knowledge of other cultures by getting to know someone whose culture is different from yours, learn about Kwanza, Cinco de Mayo, Chinese New Year, or Greek, Italian, Indian, Asian cultural holidays, or volunteer to read to a senior citizen of a culture other than your own.

Experience:
1. Outline a large circle on a flip chart or a large piece of paper. Draw lines to divide the circle into four equal parts. Label each part with a different cultural characteristic such as dress, traditions, celebrations and holidays.

CREATIVELY EXPLORING

2. Ask your child to think of a friend or neighbor from a different country. Instruct children to draw or write at least two different cultural characteristics that are different from their family culture. Tape their cultural characteristic to the appropriate section on the circle.
3. When the circle is completed, look at the characteristics that differentiate them from one another and discuss the similarities and differences.

Share:
1. How is your culture similar to another culture?
2. How is your culture different from another culture?

Process:
1. What surprised you about the similarities of the cultures?
2. What surprised you about the differences of the cultures?

Generalize:
1. What did you learn about your culture?
2. What did you learn about a different culture?

Analyze:
1. What can you do to help someone from a different culture feel welcome?
2. What can you share with others about different cultures?

Characteristics of Cultures

Directions: Write the culture characteristics in the boxes using words from the word list.

Word List

religion	values	customs
language	behaviors	norms

Activity 4: Using Good Manners to Show Respect

Objective: Your child will create a "Golden Rule" mobile and discuss using good manners.

CREATIVELY EXPLORING

Materials Needed:
- Coat hanger for each child
- Yarn or string, 6" lengths, 8 per child
- Paper, cut into 4" squares, 8 per child
- Hole punch
- Markers

Background:
Respectful people are courteous, considerate, and polite to others. There are numerous ways to show respect for others. Practicing good manners is a positive way to be respectful to others. Using good manners shows that you respect others. It also shows that you care about others' feelings. By using good manners, you are treating other people the way you would like them to treat you. Make it a point to do and say kind things that make people feel good rather than negative things that make people feel bad. It is always right to use good manners – when you know you are asking for something, saying "thank you" says I appreciate what has been given, while "I'm sorry" says you know you did something wrong. Others welcome the company of considerate people who are thoughtful, kind and caring. Considerate people help others without being asked, and are polite. They compliment others when they perform kind acts and listen to their classmates without interrupting them, follow the school and home rules. Good manners and politeness at school, while at play, at church, and during meals is very important and valued by your classmates, friends, and others around you.

Experience:
1. Children will create a mobile using the word "rule." Give your child eight large squares. On four of the squares, ask them to write the word RULE, one letter per square. Punch a hole in the top and bottom of each square. Tie one length of yarn or string to the bottom of

the coat hanger. Loop the bottom of the string through the top of a letter square and then tie a knot. Continue until all letter cards are secured to the coat hanger in the correct order. Tie the other four pieces of the yarn or string to the bottom holes of the cards.
2. Ask children to draw pictures showing "golden rule" situations on the four remaining squares. Punch a hole in the top of each card and tie the cards to the letter cards, one per letter to complete the mobile.

Share:
1. Why is it important to show others that you respect them?
2. Share a school situation that illustrated respect for a classmate?

Process:
1. What are some things we can do to show we respect others?
2. Name a respectful act that you received from a friend.

Generalize:
1. What happened at school when you did not show respect for others?
2. Can you think of how you felt when a friend did not use good manners?

Analyze:
1. What things do you want classmates to do to show respect for you?
2. How have you treated family members with respect?

CREATIVELY EXPLORING

Caring Actions to Show Respect

Directions: Using the word list, circle the hidden words in the puzzle.

Word List

Kindness	loyal	forgiving
Concerned	helping	emotional

	1	2	3	4	5	6	7	8	9	10	11	12	13	14	15	16	17
1	U	K	A	R	S	O	P	C	X	T	U	K	L	M	R	D	V
2	F	T	N	G	U	F	U	N	B	R	A	I	N	W	S	O	H
3	I	Q	Y	Z	A	I	B	I	L	M	A	D	P	E	O	E	N
4	I	L	E	M	O	T	I	O	N	A	L	M	A	P	O	D	E
5	F	O	R	G	I	V	I	N	G	L	J	E	U	A	R	S	M
6	R	K	I	N	D	N	E	S	S	D	V	F	T	N	G	E	Q
7	C	H	Y	Z	A	I	U	W	S	O	H	I	B	N	J	E	U
8	O	E	O	P	C	X	T	U	K	A	R	S	O	P	C	X	T
9	N	L	U	K	L	M	R	D	V	F	T	N	G	U	F	U	N
10	C	P	B	R	A	I	N	W	S	O	H	I	Q	Y	Z	A	I
11	E	E	B	I	L	M	A	D	P	E	O	E	N	I	L	M	A
12	R	R	P	O	D	E	L	J	E	U	L	A	R	S	M	R	D
13	N	S	V	F	T	N	G	E	Q	Y	O	Z	A	I	U	W	S
14	E	O	H	I	B	N	J	E	U	O	Y	P	C	X	T	U	K
15	D	A	R	S	O	P	C	X	T	U	A	K	L	M	R	D	V
16	F	T	N	G	U	F	U	N	B	R	L	A	I	N	W	S	O
17	H	I	Q	Y	Z	A	I	B	I	L	M	A	D	P	E	O	E
	1	2	3	4	5	6	7	8	9	10	11	12	13	14	15	16	17

Activity 5: Complimentary Caring Table

Objective: Your child will practice one method of illustrating caring for others.

DR. SHIRLEY B. MCNEILL

Materials Needed:
- Two apples
- Knife

Background:
Caring means being just as concerned about someone else as you are about yourself. Caring people give to others, show gratitude, are compassionate, and show their concern for others in tangible ways. Caring about others can be shown in many ways. One way to show that you care is through your words. Some positive words that you could say to your friends at the appropriate times are: thank you, please, and I'm sorry. Your brother, sister, mother, father, teacher, friends, relatives, and all people need to give and receive caring. In addition to words, caring can be shown in a variety of other ways such as kind acts, giving compliments, sharing, helping, listening, forgiving, or treating others the way you want to be treated. One can also show caring by listening to others and finding out about their values, cultures, beliefs, and priorities. If each and every one of us took a little time each day to care about someone else, we would make our world a better place to live for ourselves, our families, and our friends.

Experience:
1. Sit facing each other. Hold the apple in the air, ask your child to compliment you since you are holding the apple.
2. Take one apple and say something mean to it (Examples--"I hate you." "I don't want to be around you.") and drop it to the floor. Do this about four times.
3. Cut that apple in half and lay it in the center of the table allowing it to turn brown. Discuss what happened to the apple and explain that when people are treated poorly their attitude toward others can become negative.

CREATIVELY EXPLORING

Share:
1. How would you feel if you heard mean words from your family and friends?
2. Why were the complimentary words easier to receive than the mean words?

Process:
1. Have you ever thought that some people feel bruised like that apple, because they've heard mean words often?
2. How can the words we say make people feel like that apple?

Generalize:
1. When was the last time you said something nice to someone?
2. Can you think of a time when someone was mean to you or hurt your feelings?

Analyze:
1. How will you act differently in the future to your classmates or parents?
2. Why is it important to be kind and caring to others?

Sharing Complimentary Actions

Directions: Write the actions of caring people using the word bank.

Word Bank:

forgiving	listening	caring
fairness	kindness	sharing

DR. SHIRLEY B. MCNEILL

Activity 6: Caring for Friends

Objective: Children will identify caring ways to be good friends.

Materials Needed:
- A large mixing bowl
- Blank address labels
- Black marker

Background: Friendships matter. People who learn early to make and keep friends tend to engage in fewer risky behaviors, have fewer mental health problems, and recover from illnesses faster than the friendless. A friend is someone who plays with you, sits with you at lunch, cares how you feel, says kind things to you, shares your interests, willingly helps you, understands your moods, is dependable, and keeps your secrets.Friendships help one to make

CREATIVELY EXPLORING

connections to others, adjust to school, provide a connection to a supportive network, and learn important social skills. A friendship also encourages a sense of competence, buffers the hardships of day to day experiences, and enhances self-esteem. Being a friend should be a positive experience that presents valuable lessons for future healthy relationships. Some of the components of developing friendship include giving support, sensitivity, and loyalty. For young children a core of friends provides them with play mates, learning partners, sharing and growing cohorts. Positive relationships with friends and family are important to emotional development and future academic success.

Experience:
1. Prepare a list of adjectives-both positive and negative and write them on the address labels. Words like hitting, teasing, whining, tattling, complaining, gloomy, politeness, patient, loyal, kindness, helpful, fun, supportive, sharing, dependable, caring, understanding, sincere, thoughtful, loving, honest, trustworthy, and respectful.
2. Ask your child to tell you what is a recipe, then discuss what happens if a wrong ingredient is put in a recipe for a cake.
3. Remind them that when we make bad choices we often ruin our chances of making friends too. There are ingredients that go into good friendships and we're going to play a game to find good ingredients in our friendships.
4. Separate the words. Read words aloud and have the children to determine if they go into or outside of the friendship mixing bowl.
5. Pull 3-5 words out- one at a time out of the mixing bowl-ask children to tell why it is in the bowl.

Share:
1. Ask your child to name all of the words that describe one of their friends.
2. Share which words describes them, give examples to support your description.

Process:
1. Which friend ingredient is most important?
2. Share a friend ingredient that is most important to my mother and father.

Generalize:
1. Discuss a pleasing gesture made by one of your friends last week.
2. Tell your mother what she did yesterday that pleased you.

Analyze:
1. Tell what new things you will do to be a better friend to your favorite classmate.
2. Did you notice someone at school, home, or someplace else being a good friend?

CREATIVELY EXPLORING

Activities Friends Enjoy

Directions: Write the things that friends do together in the boxes using the word bank.

Word Bank

talk	play	lunch	listen
laugh	share	cry	

Activity 7: Responsibly Handling Bullying

Objective: Your child will understand why others bully and identify strategies to cope with bullying.

Materials Needed
- Paper
- Crayons

Background:
Bullying is a very old problem, some people were bullied in elementary school over 40 years ago. Bullying is still a serious problem for many children who are just starting to school and others that have been in school for a while. Usually when a child bullies, it's because he or she is unhappy at home and do not have a safe, supportive, and helpful home environment. They are probably experiencing feelings of: anger, hurt, not being loved, helpless, or experiencing a feeling of weakness at home. They are acting out their learned behavior derived from siblings and or parents. Some may have self-esteem or personal defense issues. When faced with bullying, try the following: stay calm and do not react defensively to comments; talk quietly or use humor; turn the negative into a positive by reframing. For example, if someone says something negative about your backpack, respond with "thanks for noticing my backpack"; if someone is teasing you and makes a negative comment-respond with "so what", this is my backpack, not yours. If the bullying or teasing continues, report them to your teacher, volunteer, or your parent immediately. Remember that you are special, loved and deserve respect from your peers.

Experience:
1. Define bullying and discuss why some children bully. Ask your child, "What does it mean to be brave?" After listening to the responses, explain that being brave

CREATIVELY EXPLORING

   means a lot of different things, such as doing something in a courageous, fearless manner or saying "No" to someone who is trying to get you to do something that you know is wrong.
2. Explain that it is okay to be scared sometimes and brave people get scared, too; being brave means that you try not to let those fears control how you live or act.
3. Give your child paper and crayons. Have them draw a picture showing a time where they were afraid but decided to be brave.

Share:
1. Share a time when you were scared and brave at the same time?
2. How can you act brave when you are afraid of something?

Process:
1. How can someone be hurt by a bully?
2. What new strategies will you use when being bullied?

Generalize:
1. How can you prevent becoming a bully or victim of a bully?
2. How can you support others who are being bullied?

Analyze:
1. What are some brave things you can do in the future?
2. Next time you get afraid of something, what can you do to overcome that fear?

RESPONSIBLE ACTIONS

Directions: Place the responsible actions words in alphabetical order on the lines below the word list.

Word List

Persistence   keep trying
accountability   reliability
plan actions   self-control
self-discipline   excel

1. _____
2. _____
3. _____
4. _____
5. _____
6. _____
7. _____
8. _____

CREATIVELY EXPLORING

Activity 8: Confidently Setting Goals

Objective: Your child will reflect on their talents and set goals for the future.

Materials Needed:
- Magazines (2 or 3)
- Construction paper
- Glue
- Scissors
- Paper
- Pencil

Background:
Confidence is an inner strength that gives one the will to try new things, learn new skills, and meet new people. Some have described it as trust and reliance in self. Confidence gives us the courage to resist the feelings of fear, which provides one with the capacity to confront new challenges. Confidence is a lot like self-esteem, it's situational, and not present in all phases of our lives at the same level. Your favorite animated caricatures including Chuck E Cheese and Clifford the big red dog exhibit confidence by walking and talking with assurance. They are happy, enthused, creative, playful, and outgoing. When you feel confident or positive about something, you will exhibit some of those same traits. When you are not feeling as confident as desired, consider improving your confidences by thinking about things you do well, contributions you make to help your parents and friends, and your special qualities that makes you unique. There are many ways to build your confidence including setting and accomplishing goals. Goals are plans that you have decided to give time, resources, and effort toward accomplishing. Goals can be short term meaning they will be accomplished in a day or two or long term to be accomplished in two or more years. Most successful athletes

work hard and long hours to obtain their goals, they build skills and confidence slowly, a little at the time.

Experience:
1. Your child will cut pictures or word phrases out of magazines that represent their personal goals for the future based on their interests and abilities. Then ask them to glue the pictures or word phrases to the construction paper to make a "Future Me" collage.
2. Number and display each collage.
3. Give children the opportunity to write down whom they think each "Future Me" collage belongs to based on the talents of their peers.

Share:
1. Describe how your collage looks.
2. What words could you not find to complete your "Future Me" collage?

Process:
1. What did you learn about your interests and talents?
2. Why is it important to start thinking about your interests and abilities now?

Generalize:
1. Name the special abilities and interests of your mother and father.
2. Name the special abilities and interests of your siblings or friends?

Analyze:
1. What abilities and interests does your hero possess?
2. What abilities does your favorite relative living in another state possess?

CREATIVELY EXPLORING

Building Confidence

Directions: Figure out the confidence code by placing a letter on the line to solve the riddle: This is something we can do in many ways to recognize, acknowledge and address your own needs. Actions may include things to pamper and treat yourself special such as: recording things that are unique about you.

___ ___ ___ ___ ___ ___   ___ ___ ___ ___

24 39 1 39 37 1 3   28 3 34 27

17=A	2=K	30=H
29=B	34=L	19=V
10=C	8=M	33=W
16=D	24=N	32=X
3=E	4=O	12-Y
27=F	6=P	36=Z
31=G	14=Q	1=R
28=S	37=U	39=T

Child/Parent Activities

1. Help your child learn responsibility by volunteering as a team or as a family. Share your feeling with each other about the volunteer experience, set goals, evaluate them and modify them for the future.

2. Assist and involve your child in increasing their comfort level in making decisions by goal-setting, making choices, and solving problems. Start with something fun like deciding on what your family will do to celebrate their birthday.

3. Attend and actively participate in multicultural festivals

and events, discuss with children the differences and similarities in other cultures.

4. Encourage your child to play fair, take turns, share with others, and appropriately use "thank you" and "please".

5. Expose your child to different ethnic restaurants, and ask them to write a restaurant review. You might be surprised at some of the things they notice.

6. If your child is being bullied or teased at school, provide opportunities for role playing that help him/her practice making positive choices to counteract putdowns while improving their confidence.

7. Transmit hope and optimism to your child by putting tragedies and national disasters in context. Make an effort to listen patiently and empathetically to your child's concerns and fears. Discuss current events and their dreams and plans for the future often.

8. Since a child's need for acceptance and approval is deep, make it a point to praise your child's character rather than their behavior. Compliment your child on characteristics and actions that exhibit qualities such as attentiveness, creativity, compassion, dependability, diligence, enthusiasm, flexibility, forgiveness, faith, gentleness, generosity, gratefulness, humility, initiative, loyalty, and truthfulness.

9. Attitudes toward money will determine how a person values and uses money in their life. Assist your child in tracking their spending habits by helping them to realize that there is an inflow and outflow of money. Supply them with three piggy banks: one bank for saving, one for spending for self, and the third for

CREATIVELY EXPLORING

spending for special occasions, such as Christmas. Encourage them to divide allowances or birthday and other monetary gifts between the three banks.

10. Learning styles vary for children. Whenever possible, use a variety of teaching methods with your child to promote character development. If you want your child to learn honesty, demonstrate honest behaviors at all times. Speak honestly, show your child examples of honest acts; read stories about honest people to your child and describe people who exhibit honest qualities; explain what acts are involved in being honest; and reinforce honest practices by complimenting your child when they exhibit honest traits.

CHARACTER WORDS DEFINED

Character: An individual's moral disposition including the sum total of personality traits, qualities and preferences. Usually when one is considered to have character, it is referring to good character and generally means that a person is admired because of sound and ethical behavior.

Caring: An emotional response resulting in the act of showing others concern, consideration, and kindness in a way they value.

Confidence: Believing in self and one's ability to learn and be successful in new experiences.

Citizenship: Active participation, involvement, and contribution to improve one's community while honoring and respecting authority and the law.

Culture: The customs, art, and ways of doing things for a certain group of people.

CREATIVELY EXPLORING

Fairness: Following the same rules for everyone in the same situation.

Honesty: Telling the truth, and practicing truthfulness, sincerity, and openness.

Respect: To show value to someone through the use of consideration, positive actions, attitudes, and gestures.

Responsibility: Doing your fair share and being accountable, while managing your behaviors, feelings, and attitudes while contributing to others and society.

Sharing: Giving someone a part of, or permission to use something that belongs to you.

Trust: Believing that someone is honest, dependable, reliable, and possess integrity.

Trustworthiness: Deserving of trust of others as a result of honesty, loyalty, building a sound reputation, and having the courage to do right even if others are doing wrong.

Valuing Diversity: Respecting and accepting differences of others, including: beliefs, lifestyles, height, ethnicity, sexuality, culture, age, gender, and religion without prejudice.

REFERENCES

Austin, Phyllis. 2005. *Parents, The Power Behind Your Child's Success: Unlocking Your Child's Full Potential Cultivating Your Child's Uniqueness Helping Your Child Succeed in School.* Decatur, GA*: Austin Reprographics.*

Battle-Baldwin, Jean. 2003. *Parenting Matters: Parent Educator's Guide,* Greensboro, NC. North Carolina A&T State University.

Barnes, B.J., and Hill, Shirley. 1982. *Young Children and Their Families.* Lexington, Mass., and Toronto: D.C. Heath and Company.

Barth, Patte, and Mitchell, Ruth. 1992. *Smart Start: Elementary Education for the 21st Century.* Golden, CO: North American Press.

Beaty, Janice. 1994. *Observing Development of the Young Child.* Englewood Cliffs, NJ, and Columbus, OH: Merrill.

Bredekamp, S., and Cople, C. 1997. *Developmentally Appropriate Practice in Early Childhood Programs.* Washington, DC: National Association for the Education of Young Children.

Bickart, Toni, Dodge, Diane, Jablon, Judy. 1997. *What Every Parent Needs To Know About 1st, 2nd, & 3rd Grades.* Naperville, IL: Sourcebooks.

Canfield, Jack, and Siccone, Frank. 1995. *101 Ways to Develop Student Self-esteem and Responsibility.* Boston, London, Toronto, Sydney, Tokyo, and Singapore: Allyn and Bacon.

Cartledge, G., and Milburn, J. 1995. *Teaching Social Skills To Children and Children: Innovative Approaches.* Needham Heights, Mass: Allyn and Bacon.

Coleman, Paul. 2000. *How to Say It to Your Kids: The Right Words to Solve Problems, Soothe Feelings, and Teach Values.* Paramus, NJ: Prentice Hall Press.

Communications, Sunburst, 1998. *Parent & Child: Guidance & Health Educational Media.* Pleasantville, NY: Sunburst Company.

Day, Barbara. 1988. *Early Childhood Education: Creative Learning Activities.* New York: McMillan Publishing Company.

Domar, Alice. 2000.*Self-Nurture: Learning to Care for Yourself as Effectively as You Care For Everyone Else:* New York, NY, Penguin Group.

Duval, Lynn. 1994. *Respecting Our Differences: Minneapolis, MN;* Free Spirit Publishing.

Einon, Dorothy. 1985. *Play with a Purpose.* New York: Random House. Feldman, Beverly. 1987. *Kids Who Succeed.* NY: Rawson Associates.

Exceptional Children's Assistance Center. 2002. *Parent Partners Empower.* Davidson, NC: US Department of Education, Special Education Programs.

Innes, Dick. 2002. *Character Counts, ACTS International Ministries. Arcadia,* CA: ACTS International.

Leman, Kevin, 1992. *The Birth Order Book: Why You Are The Way You Are*: New York, NY, Dell Publishing Company.

Krueger, Caryl. 1994. *365 Ways to Love Your Child:* Nashville, TN, *Abingdon Press.*

Magee, Trish.1998. *Raising A Happy, Confident, Successful Child: 12 Lessons to help Parents Grow*: Holbrook, MA, Adams Media Corporation.

Moore, Diane. 2005. *Parenting the Heart of Your Child.* Minneapolis, MN: Bethany House Publishers.

Josephson, Michael. 2006. *Resources: Making Ethical Decisions: The Six Pillars of Character.* Aspen, CO: Josephson Institute of Ethics.

Raatma, Lucia. 2000. *Character Education: Courage; Character Education: Consideration; Character Education: Responsibility:* Minneapolis, MN: Bridgestone Books.

Turner, Bud, Turner, Susan. 2000. *Ready to Use: Pre-Sport Skills Activities Program:* Paramus, NJ: Parker Publishing Company.

Turner, Jeffrey & Helms, Donald. 1995. *Life Span Development:* Fort Worth, TX, Philadelphia, San Diego, NY, Orlando, Austin, San Antonio, Toronto, Montreal. London, Sydney, Tokyo: Harcourt Brace College Publishers.